# SO YOU THINK YOU'RE A SKATEBOARDER?

# SO YOU THINK YOU'RE A SKATEBOARDER?

## 45 tales from the streets and the skatepark

### Alex Irvine
### with illustrations by Paul Parker

DOG 'N' BONE

Published in 2014 by Dog 'n' Bone Books
An imprint of Ryland Peters & Small Ltd
20–21 Jockey's Fields        519 Broadway, 5th Floor
London WC1R 4BW          New York, NY 10012

www.rylandpeters.com

10 9 8 7 6 5 4 3 2 1

Text © Alex Irvine 2014
Design and illustration © Dog 'n' Bone Books 2014

A CIP catalog record for this book is available from
the Library of Congress and the British Library.

ISBN: 978 1 909313 43 9

Illustration: Paul Parker
Design: Wide Open Studios

For digital editions, visit
www.cicobooks.com/apps.php

Printed in China

# CONTENTS

Introduction 6

## The Skaters

# INTRODUCTION

**So you think you're a skateboarder? Looks easy, right? I mean it's only standing sideways on a board, how hard can that be?!**

Well, for starters, there's a whole new language to learn: you're going to have to know how to differentiate between a heelflip and a kickflip if you want to avoid looking like a douche.

Next, where do you get your deck? Are you going to go out and buy a brand-new setup or are you going to meet someone who skates and borrow their board to see if it really is all that easy?

Then there's the question of where to go to do it. Should you be a park rat or tough it out on the streets?

Are you going to turn up for your first session wearing every pad you can find that might protect your precious skin, or are you going to take some falls and really find out how sore learning to skate can be?

Regardless of what you want to do and where you want to do it, you're going to have to figure out where you fit in, who you're going to make friends with, and what bits of skateboarding you really care about.

Then there are cliques within cliques you're going to have to try to recognize, alongside all the bravado, insanity, weirdos, assholes, and good guys you'll encounter on a regular basis. It's great!

The following pages hopefully go some way toward helping you realize whether or not you're cut out for this bone-crunching, attitude-filled pastime and precisely where you fit in if you do.

Skate or die, bro!

# PHOTOGRAPHER

**Nerdy, weighed down by more camera equipment that can possible be necessary, broke... Is the life of a skateboard photographer really all it's cracked up to be?**

These days it seems everyone's a photographer, which can make the decision to try and become a professional exponent of the art a little more fraught with the risk of financial ruin. But hey, your mother says you've got an eye for a picture and your dad's got an old camera you can borrow. How hard can it be, right?

Deciding to devote your life to making it as a photographer can be a choice not that unlike the decision to join a monastery: long hours, no money, and, until you're raking in the cash at least, long bouts of celibacy and general social reclusiveness.

Most photographers begin their career shooting their friends, which, unless your crew is amazingly talented, means wasting thousands of rolls of film or—as is more likely these days— hours of battery power filling up memory cards with unsalable crap. But they're willing test subjects and you share a small room in a damp apartment with them, so it's perfect.

Waiting at the bottom of a set of stairs for hours on end while your gnarliest friend tries his hardest move, predicting he will land each attempt "this try," should leave you plenty of time to contemplate the important things in your chosen life. Unfortunately, the smell from that puddle of piss you're kneeling in is distracting you so much that your mind wanders and you miss the trick. As your friend rides away into glory, you also feign joy, quietly muttering "Yeah bro!" along with all your other mates, secretly knowing you blew the shot and he's going to have to come back and try it again another day. And guess what—it's your fault.

It's not all bad, though. I mean, sucking it up and getting out there again beats what you'd be doing otherwise: waiting around for your friends to get their lazy asses out of bed, trawling the Internet for tips on editing your work, scouring eBay for cheap replacements for all your uninsured gear that broke when it got hit with that stray board, and generally panicking about how this career choice is ever going to pay the rent.

Eventually, when the planets align and fortune shines its light on you, you're going to have an image that you're proud of. Your unreliable flash fired that time, your friend pulled his trick, you got the timing right, and you didn't accidentally delete the file when you got home. Now it's time to sit down in front of that borrowed computer with your ancient version of Photoshop and do your thing. But that's only if the back pain from carrying that gear around all day isn't kicking in in earnest.

Maybe, if you're lucky, this photo will make you some money; maybe this one could really kick-start your career; maybe it will propel your gnarly friend into stardom and you were there with him when he was a nobody. Maybe someone poached your shot on their smartphone and blew out your prized image on Instagram, or worse, maybe the trick been one-upped before you even get the chance to try and sell it. If, by some miracle, the photo makes it to print, you can invoice the magazine, and in a month you'll have enough money to pay back the cash you borrowed from your friends when you were broke the other month. But the phone is ringing, it's your friend, and he has a spot he wants to skate. You'd better hurry up!

# THE STONER

**You might think you have priorities in life, but the Stoner has real priorities. A need. A need for weed.**

Remember when you were younger and you were trying to fit in and be cool? Remember what was cool? Smoking was cool. And disobeying your parents, acting stupid, not washing your hair, and being lazy were even cooler. Then you had your first toke of a joint and you realized all this rebelliousness could be condensed into one hard-to-get-hold-of and expensive plastic baggy.

Well, that was a few years ago now, but you never really bothered to kick the habit: it makes you feel chill, it makes boring things funny, it stops you worrying about that tax return you should have filed and, most importantly, it helps you skate. No, really.

The title of "Stoner" gets bandied around fairly readily in the world of skateboarding, but it can be a pretty ambiguous term. Like autism, it's more of a scale that you may find yourself on. To the one side is the Bill Clinton "I never inhaled it" dabbler and to the other extreme is the "What year was I born again?" legalize-it lifer.

So, how do you know if you're officially a Stoner or just someone who smokes the occasional bit of weed here and there? There are a few clues here that might help you figure out where you sit on the scale.

## You have a weed-leaf motif on your grip tape

This seems like a fairly obvious one but, contradictory to what the general public might believe, this could denote the exact opposite. Not that kids are thinking ironically when they order that heinous sheet of grip to daub their deck, rather that they don't understand exactly what it means to iconize the weed leaf. True Stoners are too busy being stoned to bother hunting down hash-leaf splattered garms.

### You have a Bob Marley shirt or rasta tri-color wristbands on

See above.

### It's 9am and you're already stoned

This one is a trick! Everyone knows real Stoners don't get out of bed before noon.

### You're rolling a joint at the first skatespot of the day

Okay, you're probably a Stoner, at least you're getting pretty close, but it's only one spot and it's only one joint. The thing about being a Stoner is you've developed such a high (sorry) tolerance that your intake has gone through the roof, so a true Stoner will be found rolling up at every spot, chasing that elusive high. While this habit might punctuate the flow of sessions with a lot of sitting around smoking and hunting for snacks, it still doesn't mean you've completely blown your chances of becoming the world's best. Here's why: a lot of the world's best skateboarders are Stoners. A lot of the best skateboarding has been done stoned. By Stoners. So, you're pretty sure you're one of these rare, high-level functioning Stoners, but how do you know for sure? You probably won't. You probably never will because you're so stoned. One of the quirks of our little spart (a pioneering portmanteau of sport and art) is that you can get so out of it that you can't tell exactly how well you're doing it. You know you're doing it and you know you're enjoying doing it but... Hey, has anyone got any papers?

# GRIZZLED 80S VETERAN

**Cautious, well-fed, and armed with strong opinions and an even stronger sense of self-importance, older skaters can be a skatepark's most annoying user group.**

Until recently, these advocates of the middle-aged shred were a fairly rare sight, mainly due to the fact that there simply were no older skaters because skateboarding itself is so young. Unfortunately, the halcyon days of a youthful, attitude-filled sport are well and truly behind us. Now, pretty much every skatepark will have at least one of these gray-haired know-it-alls in attendance, and the following rules of thumb will make it easier to identify exactly who we're dealing with.

The first clue to identifying your typical elder skatesman is that he will probably have a board from skateboarding's past— a time that he sees as the defining era of the sport. It will come as no surprise that he is more likely to be interested in remembering the way so-and-so did that long-forgotten trick back in the 80s than what crazy new move Nyjah Huston just did down the Hollywood High 16. The key thing to note here is that, in addition to being non-progressive as a viewpoint, this nostalgic lilt is always hypocritically rose-tinted. The 80s weren't purely a good time for skateboarding, they were also a time responsible for massive egos, fluorescent Lycra, and streetplants. Show me a guy who loves the 80s so much he dresses like a heyday Christian Hosoi every Sunday morning, and I'll take off my trilby and eat it.

Wait a minute, what are those weird plastic things either side of that Jason Jesse Neptune reissue he's got carefully positioned on the deck of the ramp, angled just right, so that the pristine graphic is pointed toward everyone? Why those are called rails. But whatever you do, don't ask him about them, unless you enjoy being bored into a coma while he expands on the benefits of riding the Variflex-branded ones he's using. And, as you can see, he also wears pads, the kind with the all-over cheetah print that his other 80s hero always wore. That's fair enough, because his bones aren't what they used to be and if he breaks his elbow, then his job at the data-input firm is definitely screwed. Can you imagine the embarrassment that comes when a man of his years has to explain exactly how he screwed up his arm to his guffawing colleagues who think skateboarding's just for kids.

If you're lucky enough, you'll find him unable to bend your ear about the good old days thanks to a full mouth, having just tucked into the home-packed lunch and Thermos of coffee that his wife makes for him and his son. The four-year-old boy has been forced to take up skateboarding thanks to dad's determination; Pop skated, so he's damn well sure his kid will, too.

If nothing else, at least clinging on to his youth gets him out of the house for a few hours every Sunday. To be fair, it's the only thing likely to help shift a bit of that beer gut all those pints at the local have endowed him with.

# FREESTYLER

## A long time ago in a galaxy far, far, away, Freestylers ruled the skateboarding universe. Now they just own all the companies.

Often one of the toughest things to master the first time you set foot on a skateboard is the darty, backward-and-forward motion that occurs through having no brakes. Type "falling off sk8board" into any search engine on the Internet and the top hits will be people grappling with this lateral-motion conundrum. There's good reason so much of it is recorded and put online, because the results are as predictable as a granny at a wedding deciding that she's going to dance to this song while standing on the table.

This inability to move forward is something most skateboarders have overcome and long since forgotten they ever struggled with. As a result, the comedy value of some inexperienced person falling down is replaced with a kind of knowing warning to be careful. To the general public, this skateboard thing's just a toy, so most of these warnings are disregarded, macho-style, and subsequently a lot of members of the public eat tarmac, hard. If you're new to the skateboard world and this bone-crunching encounter with gravity sounds all too familiar, worry not. There is an entire ancient world of static skateboarding to be discovered and it goes by the name of Freestyle.

Now this is a style not to be confused with the art of adlibbing within hip hop, and it couldn't be further from this modern act of cool if it tried.

Freestylers are more like the kids locked in their bedroom writing their own computer programs, rather than rappers recording their experiences "in the street." Cool freestyle is not. This is the thick-rimmed-glasses-and-mouth-full-of-train-tracks face of skating. If you're choosing this path, be prepared to be ostracized, outcast, and ignored; not in a nasty way, more in an embarrassing-dad-dance kind of way, or the-uncle-that-nobody-talks-about kind of way. The Freestylers are the social outcasts of a "sport" full of social outcasts, so you can kind of imagine just how lonely a life you're picking.

The traditional dress of the Freestyler used to be short shorts, vest, headbands, and taped-up thumbs (to stop the grip tape hurting your hands when you danced around on the board), and to be honest, the species is so near extinction that I'm at a loss as to what they look like now— I'm guessing the same. The boards Freestylers use are often pretty weird, more like planks of wood than anything you'll find in a skateshop. I don't even know where you'd go to get one these days. Freestylers probably have to make them themselves.

Should you be lucky enough to meet someone who shares your passion for stationary performances (and well done for finding them, really well done), then you'll have a fraternal bond stronger than in any other aesthetic of skateboarding. And you'll be deserving of the ego boost gained by knowing that Freestylers gave birth to modern street skateboarding, that Rodney Mullen is a genius, and that the guys who were really nerdy and really, really good at it own all the skateboard companies anyway.

# THE GLUTTON

**Sometimes you get the bull, sometimes the bull gets you, then repeatedly stamps your body into the ground, leaving you writhing in agony. Similarly, skateboarding can be a pretty cruel mistress: one minute you're up, king of your world, the next you're a pile, writhing on the floor grabbing your shin and trying not to cry. You should try and get used to being embarrassed, dejected, and beaten, because it's not like it ever stops happening. It's part of the game... Wuss.**

The spirit to get back up and try again burns brighter in some of us than others. Some of us will get a shinner and have to take the rest of the day off, but there are those who will just not be stopped. Like a cyborg sent from the future who needs your clothes, your boots, and your motorcycle, they'll just keep going.

The Glutton for punishment will often be found going big because that's his trade: the show stopper. The Glutton for punishment isn't going to roll the dice on any old trick on any old terrain, his battles for glory will only take place on the most scary, inconceivably brutal, or outright insane obstacles. If you're going to ruin your body, you might as well get some props out of the deal.

The Glutton has chosen to dice with death, day in, day out, and when it goes wrong, he's ready. He knows he's going down, and he knows he's going to go down hard, but, unless he's snapped his neck or broken the spot to pieces, somehow he'll find the willpower to get back up and try it again.

This guts and glory approach to stuntwork leads to a few defeats here and there—a few "I'll be backs"—but win or lose, local skaters are always going to talk about the day when the Glutton rolled through town. Any defeats will be overshadowed by the folklore he generated just by trying something so insane for hours on end, because watching people eat shit is memorable and everyone loves to see a slam or two. And when the Glutton wins, when he beats the spot and rides triumphantly away from a battle, the rewards are tenfold.

Regardless of this fail-safe route to glory, there are a few things to consider if you fancy yourself as one of these human punchbags. Firstly, it's going to hurt, a lot, so you might want to make sure you are prepared to take a few days off here and there. You're going to need ice packs in your freezer at all times (for all the bruises) and you will go through T-shirts at a rate of knots, so you might want to try and secure yourself a sponsor.

If you're unsure about whether or not this career in corpse-tossing is your cup of tea, why not try throwing yourself down the next set of stairs you come across and see how it feels. See you at the hospital.

# LONGBOARDER

## Size matters. That's what they say. But does it?

The Longboarder is the publicly acceptable face of skateboarding, but it may surprise you to learn that this person is not particularly loved by the kind of skateboarders (here, for the sake of argument, I'm talking about the Shortboarders) who make up the majority of the sport.

The Shortboarder may often be found chanting the mantra "Life's too short for longboarding!" at passing partakers of the long version. Thanks to clueless fashion-magazine editors and unsavvy media outlets, both skateboarding (shortboarding) and its lanky cousin get lumped into the same bag, which, as far as the public are concerned, makes us all one big, happy family. This is not the case. Not the case at all.

It's not that longboarding is hated by skaters as such, it's more of a case that it's ignored—a bit like (sticking with this played-out family metaphor) the embarrassing uncle that the rest of the family doesn't talk about. Interestingly, the main source for this animosity is that the public generally consider it OK to ride one of these boards. I can't see the reason for this other than that most Norms seem to be able to stand on them, perhaps purely as there's more board under their feet. Some of these nerds can actually steer one of them.

From the office worker to the girl with the ethnic-pattern poncho that reeks of patchouli oil, longboarding crosses the boundaries that regular skateboarding is happy to avoid. I suppose the boundless accessibility of longboarding is the key to its popularity. You don't have to go to a skatepark or street spot to do it; you don't have to worry about learning any tricks; you can do it in Crocs or brogues or whatever it is Longboarders wear on their feet—all these things appeal to Joe Public.

To the Normals, longboarding gives a taste of skateboarding without any pesky social detraction, attitude, or baggy clothes. I mean, to most skaters, the thought of dragging your board around in between the flat bits of street while slurping on an iced coffee, listening to Dido, stopping to step—rather than ollie—up curbs, and arranging skate dates with your crusty other half (don't forget your acoustic guitar!) on a Sunday just ain't going to cut it.

Still, not everyone who rides a longboard can be called amateurish, that would be too harsh, even from a confessed hater such as myself. After all, not everyone is shit-footing his or her way down the bus lane of life dressed like the teacher of a circus school. Some Longboarders get respect from the skate community. There are exceptions.

Some guys take it very seriously, like the ones who aren't afraid to take a risk or two and bomb the hills at a hundred miles an hour with their hands behind their backs. These guys cannot be called anything but ballsy. And that's in keeping with the essence of rebellion skateboarding purports to have.

There are also those who somehow manage to skate these oversized beasts as though they were normal-sized boards; the guys who can blunt fakie mini ramps and things like that. That shit is impressive, purely on a practical level. But if you're not one of them, then sorry man, we don't want to know about it. Don't forget to say hi!

# PARK SKATER

**Preferring the smooth, reliable contours of the purpose-built park to the quirks and potholes you find in street skating, the Park Skater is a highly tuned, albeit caged animal. From the "gnarly" bowl skater covered in crap tattoos to the headphone-wearing "street-plaza" aficionado, a true Park Skater is owner of his particular terrain, the big fish in the small pond, king of his own little hill. But how can this guy afford just to hang around the local park every day? Does he even have a job?**

Many skaters will happily tell you the essence of skateboarding lies in riding the streets. The Park Skater sees things differently, either convinced that the skateboard was made to ride the curves and bumps of a moon-scaped concrete utopia, or that it's more fun to roll undisturbed on the glass-like surface of a professionally finished floor. Whatever the preferred terrain, the Park Skater knows every curve and blemish of his local park following years of repetitive movement. As a result, his trick repertoire is exceptionally impressive. Not only can he do more tricks in a session than your average skater lands in a week, but he's also insanely consistent thanks to his knowledge of the intricacies of the place. The info of where the cracks are and how slippery each section of floor is are all locked inside his mind.

The Park Skater can perform tricks pretty much on command, which comes in handy when he needs to show the new guy who's boss or wants to impress a visiting skate team with his best stunts in the hope of gaining sponsorship. Ultimately, both of these attempts at asserting himself as the ruler of the park will fail to excite anyone, skateboarding isn't really about that. The truth is he's only going to end up looking like a prick. No one likes bullies or show-offs, so leave the ego at the gate.

The main issue for any Park Skater isn't this vain peacocking or the goldfish-in-a-bowl nature of only skating within a set boundary. The problem is that by only ever skating a purpose-built facility you're going to get lazy.

The moment you arrive at a street spot and realize the world outside the park isn't glass smooth and exactly how you remember it, you're going to suck. No amount of perfecting your skill or training up on a skatepark ledge is going to do you any favors when you're faced with a pot-holed landing or janky, dog-turd-laden run-up.

Some people say that by only skating parks you sap the creative juices you need for real street skateboarding, and they may well be right. But, you know what, if you're good at park skating, there's a decent park for you to do it at, and you're happy, then who cares what anybody else says.

# STAIR FANATICS

**Skaters are attracted to stairs like college students are attracted to cheap alcohol deals and terrible pop music. Here are a couple of stair-loving types to look out for.**

## The Counter

Skateboarding's not a sport, right? Yet that doesn't mean people are going to stop trying to go one bigger than they did last time, especially where stair counting is concerned.

At the dawn of street skateboarding, I'm pretty sure the pioneers wouldn't have seen this obsession coming. It must seem ridiculous to people who don't skateboard that skaters pay that much attention to something so seemingly trivial as the number of stairs you can jump down. But going bigger, grinding longer, and upping that stair count is—in addition to being a marker for personal goals—a publicly contestable subject that is open for discussion and conjecture within skateboard circles. Granted, quantification of street spots into a set of numbers and types is useful to know. For example, your peers might want to check out your spot and this information prepares them for how high and how long it's going to be before they go there to try and one-up your trick. However, it definitely makes skaters sound a bit mad to the general public when things like stairs are discussed in the vocabulary lexicon of "big 4" or a "3-flat-3."

For skaters, the fact that the units of measurement for steps aren't standardized doesn't really seem to be of concern—they are either just big or normal. While this means always trying to go one bigger could lead to an inaccurate and debatable result, we can remind ourselves that this is skateboarding and this kind of nonsensical idiosyncrasy is fine. Still, the bigger it is, the more props you're going to get.

# The Rail Chomper

The more dangerous a handrail, the better, because it doesn't matter if it's round, square, mellow, steep, or skate stopped—nothing's going to stop the Rail Chomper getting his. Always on the lookout for somewhere new and crazy to take his rail-skating skills, a Chomper can be found fighting his inner demons at the top of stair-sets the world over.

Armed with an array of tricks that can be adapted to any variation of cold steel tubing, this guy is out to push himself even harder than a regular Stair Counter. Although there's less impact involved with rails, there's much more to risk. It's no secret that the area between a man's legs is some of the most precious flesh he possesses and, understandably, most guys go to great lengths to make sure it stays in prime condition. The mind of a Rail Chomper is at odds with man's natural instinct to protect his package thanks to the perfectly troublesome height at which most banisters are set: just that little bit higher than the length of your inside leg measurement. Constantly living with the risk of a genital-crunching slam is no mean feat and this guy has some big balls to protect. Of course, even though men's junk tends to be a little more precariously "out there," the ladies who partake must also be equipped with "big balls."

Nowadays, guys who excel in this absurd niche are taking the balancing act of rail skating to places no one ever imagined possible: round corners, toward lampposts, through kinks... even uphill. In short, the focus and attention required to successfully complete handrail maneuvers seem to appeal to a set of riders who are not only ultra-consistent and willing to risk their 'nads, but also more fearless than those guys who wrestle 'gators for a living. Some might call them insane, I call them brave!

# THE TECH GUY

**Progressive, obsessive, and patient, the Tech Guy ain't going to be put off by a few failed attempts at a new move, more likely he'll be there all day and night 'til he gets it right.**

First up: there's going to be a lot of trying if you want to be the Tech Guy. Skateboarding has a lot to do with failure—you try, you fail, and eventually, hopefully, you learn to land and roll away. It's all part of the fun.

The sense of accomplishment achieved from pulling tricks is something that can't be duplicated and the harder, gnarlier, and (to some) more tech the trick, the bigger the buzz. Tech Guys choose to take this to the extreme, forgoing the incremental stoke of landing regular tricks and instead choosing to hold out for the mother-load payoff of a full day's work. The kind of awesome feeling that waits to be reaped by doing the tricks you already know you can do, by retrying the ones you fluked that one time in the past, or maybe even by trying to pull that hard one you rolled your ankle on doesn't quite cut it for a Tech Guy. Instead, he prefers to focus the foreseeable future of his existence on perfecting that one mind-bending brain scrambler of a move.

To be a Tech Guy generally requires loose fitting clothing. Sweatpants seem to be the most popular choice as there's going to be some serious training required. This ain't a game no more and the improvement of individual muscles takes the kind of focus that most people just don't have the patience for. It's useful to have some headphones for entertainment, because you're going to be the last guy skating every session. You'll also need supplies: water for hydration and sugar for energy—you don't want anything interrupting your flow, breaking that focus.

In addition to the insane amount of dedication, the muscle memory required by the Tech Guy is as impressive as anything you're likely to see in skateboarding, but it comes at a cost. While everyone around you moves from trick to trick, from spot to spot, you're going to be stuck in the same place trying to make your trick until the filmer runs out of battery and all your mates head home for dinner. But that's fine, you're not doing it for them. This is YOUR trick.

So, you think you've got what it takes and you're pretty sure the life of the Tech Guy is the bag, but it might be worth seriously considering a few things before you try and make it your career. I mean, if you're OCD, that might help; if you're determined, that will really help; and, if you're willing to sacrifice entire days of your life to hold out for the big payload of stoke when you finally land that 360-flip nosegrind down at the skatepark, that's definitely going to help. But the thing is, unless you're insanely talented enough to be doing this nonchalantly, or styled-out slicker than the handle on Dylan Rieder's pomade-drawer, it's probably not going to bag you that spot in the next Plan B video anytime soon.

So, you know, maybe you should consider becoming a Freestyler instead.

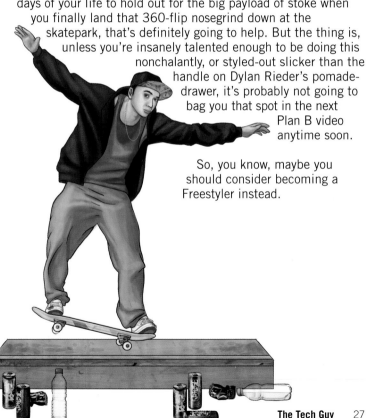

# VERT SKATER

**Chances are that this guy right here has been around a while. If he hasn't, then he's probably hanging out with dudes who have. These are the guys who ride the big stuff.**

In the 80s, vert was king; it WAS skateboarding as far as the general public was concerned. The showboating nature of vert's leading frontmen, the amplitude of the stunts they performed, and the stadium-friendly nature of the vert ramp meant it was perfect for capturing the imagination of the general public. Over a quarter of a century later and the medium still continues to capture imaginations, and vert legend Tony Hawk's draw is bigger than ever.

As a former Vert Skater, if you're thinking about dusting off that board you've still got somewhere in the attic, it might be of use to have a few reminders and pointers on exactly what's up with vert skating and its followers these days. Thankfully, for your aging body at least, people still wear pads, but if you've been off a board for the last 30 years, you're probably going to want to invest in a set that is a couple of sizes bigger than when you last climbed the steps up to the top deck of the ramp. Another thing you'll find is that there are a few more steps than there were the last time you made the walk to the top because the ramps are bigger than they were back in the day, way bigger. And bigger means faster, so you're going to want to be ready for that. Another positive is that despite the boom-and-bust state of the vert ramp, there are definitely a lot more around than when you were doing it, and these ones aren't so skinny that you're flying off the edge if you make one wrong move.

Maybe you're one of those guys who never stopped skating vert, who never lost the buzz of the aerial maneuver or allure of the acrid stench eminating from the sports bag where you keep your sweaty pads. If that's the case, you've probably got a solid friend base, because die-hard Vert Skaters who stuck with it through the 90s, when it was declared dead, are few and far between. That kind of friendship counts and these guys are the keepers of the font of knowledge. They are the walking, talking trick-a-pedia; they know the names of all the different inverts and probably the stories behind them. And they'll happily talk your ear off about it, whether you're asking or not!

It's not only old guys who skate vert, you know—their kids love it, too. And when a child is raised by a skateboard illuminati, he or she is probably going to be unstoppable in the generations to come, so prepare to be embarrassed, superseded, and, if that little guy happens to be your offspring, intensely proud.

# THE PURIST

**Skateboarding is full of guys who love to tell you they skate purely for the love of skateboarding, not for money or for fame—whether you asked them in the first place or not.**

Armed with a subscription to *Thrasher*, a beaten board, a pair of chewed-up skate shoes, and a large helping of attitude, the Purists are skateboarding's rebellious, anti-social gate keepers. They care about its history and have principles they will not compromise on. They're always happy to let you know exactly what they think about skateboarding and what's wrong with it.

To call these guys Purists may be the understatement of the century. If you don't skate, they probably don't want to know you; if your kid rides a scooter they hate you (and your kid); and if you're wearing a major sports brand's latest sneakers, they don't want to be anywhere near you.

To give these guys their credit, they are the only ones trying to keep skateboarding in a place where a lot of people's hearts loved it being: the past. They hark back to the days when wheels were extra small and pants were extra-large, when there was no money in it, when people hated you purely because you chose to ride a skateboard... Wait, these guys sound kind of bitter... I'm backing them though, I think...

The Purists are the doomsayers, the boom-bust predictors who have been circulating rumors of skateboarding's demise since the start of the millennium, probably longer. Their theory, that the big corporations who have funneled their millions into skateboarding are soon going to take them right back out again, crushing the industry in the process, has not yet come true— but they're still convinced. And no, they're not wearing a foil hat!

Sometimes it does feel like no one's listening, no one's taking them seriously, but these guys are serious. Maybe writing these ideas down on a placard and standing on a street corner warning everybody about the impending doom isn't such a bad idea. Nah, that's a waste of time, Purists don't care about any of that crap anyway. It's only about riding a skateboard and that's it. Skate or die! Skate and destroy! Don't do it!

This kind of attitude rightfully earns them respect among their peers. They are die hards, true believers, and nothing's going to change their opinion, and who can't respect stubbornness? As well as the kudos this stance affords a Purist, it also gives unwritten permission to act in certain ways. To own a dog and take it skateboarding everywhere you go, even if all it does is try and bite everyone's wheels, to get covered in tattoos (the more socially unacceptable and "core" the better), to drink beer all day, and to let everyone know that you don't give a crap, unless their crap is the crap you hate.

In the eyes of a Purist, skateboarding needs to die. It's too popular and you shouldn't bother starting. We're better of without you anyway. Now leave.

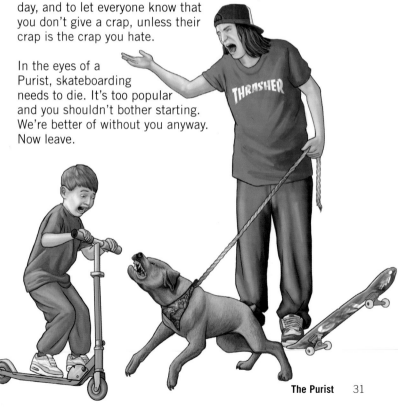

# HILL BOMBER

**Reckless, padless, loco... Hill Bombers have little regard for their own personal safety and little time for your opinion about what they're doing.**

Once you've learned to ride a skateboard, you quickly realize the faster you can go, the more exciting it is. Of course, the faster you go, the more dangerous it gets; that's exactly why it's more exciting. To the unprepared and the naive, "hill bombing," as the act of skateboarding down a steep hill is known, is nearly one hundred percent guaranteed to end in failure. Depending on the gradient of the incline you're attempting, you could be in for anything from concussion to skinned knees and even death. Sounds ominous, I know, but stick with me.

What I'm trying to reiterate is that the dudes who make this pastime a regular feature in their daily lives are not messing around. I mean, Hill Bombers know what they're doing but the rug can still be pulled out from underneath them. Now, if you're sitting there asking yourself: "What's he on about? How hard can it be to go down a hill without falling off?!," you might want to re-read the second paragraph again. And if you're still reading, here are a few things you might want to have a little think about before you step aboard this four-wheeled deathtrap.

**First thing to note:** There are no brakes.

**Second thing to note:** There are only three ways to slow down.

**Dragging your foot:** A serious faux pas if you're looking to gain respect in this field, just so you know. It's also by no means a foolproof way to avoid disaster. If you're already going too fast when you start this method, your board is going to lose you quicker than a bucking bronco ditches a two-bit redneck.

**Powersliding:** If you want to look cool and slow down, you can always try to powerslide (that is to skid your board 90 degrees sideways before returning to face forward) your way out of this out-of-control acceleration. This works well, but you might want to practice it on the flat before taking it to a really steep hill.

**Hit something:** Very effective at stopping you, but not advised.

If you can't manage any of these and fear events are turning sour, there's an absolute last resort method: try and run out. But be warned, if you're going fast this rarely works. Then again, if the other option is the dreaded speed wobbles, causing the board to judder uncontrollably, then this might be your best course of action. Do you want to jump or be pushed?

In conclusion, if you've learned how to overcome speed wobbles, you've summoned the willpower to see this thing through to the end, you've made sure your wheel nuts are all on tight, and you've triple checked the timing of the traffic lights, then with a little luck you might make it to the bottom. Just keep your fingers crossed that no one runs a red light. Please don't try this at home.

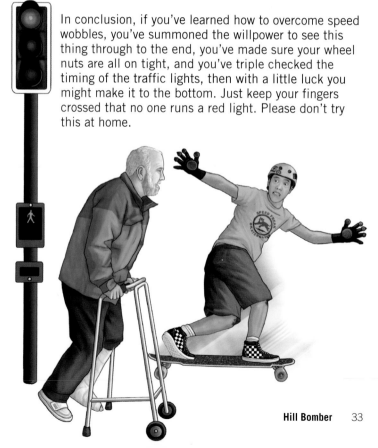

# THE PRODIGY

**Remember the Eddie Murphy film THE GOLDEN CHILD, about a kid who can save humankind? Well, imagine that, only more annoying, with less jokes, a lot less kung fu, but a lot more skateboard skills and pushy parents. That's the story of the Prodigy.**

The Prodigy is good, really good. He's been skating since he could walk, maybe even earlier. Shredding the whizz plank is probably in his genes, because these days people who used to rip it up back in the 70s, 80s, 90s, and even the 2000s have spawned children, some of whom have inherited their parents' abilities. As annoying as it can be watching someone three-foot high and less than half your age skating better than you ever will, you'd have to be a bit of an asshole to begrudge the Prodigy his fun.

The main source of jealousy toward these gifted young souls is their enhanced skill level, especially when matched with a consistency that you can never relate to. This envy is compounded because a Prodigy's skills are always progressing in leaps and bounds, not stagnating like yours have been for the last however many years. Rather than being jealous, I think it's more constructive to be hateful and spiteful. Resign yourself to the fact that they've had it too easy and that it wasn't like that in your day. Your dad never took you skating and taught you how to ollie. He wanted you to play regular sports, to learn to be a team player. If you'd had an upbringing like that, things would have been different. Right...

If hate and spite still aren't enough, you'll be happy to know there's another reason you can actively dislike these little wunderkinds: their parents. For the most part, these adults— the same ones who are driving their kids around, taking them skating, pushing them to make their mark in the "sport"—are not only actively ruining their child's chances of ever becoming big in the game, but also making it tough for the little 'un to make friends and earn the respect of co-skaters.

Think about it: if you enjoyed the freedom of skating when you were a kid, would you swap it for a childhood spent under the beady eye of your ma or pa standing on the sideline, "positively" reinforcing you to "do better," "motivating" you, or even just hanging around for the whole session? I'm guessing not. You're going to miss out on all the important stuff, like finding your own way and doing naughty shit that parents don't like you doing: cursing at security guards, eating nothing but junk food all day, or starting to smoke. You'll probably never chat up a girl in the street, trespass on a backyard pool, skate an abandoned building, bomb a hill with your buddies, or experience anything dangerous (aka fun) if you've got overbearing parents making sure you've got an ice-cold isotonic sports drink ready to go at the end of a hard training session.

So, enjoy the fact you were never that good. You may not have done it as well as them, but I bet you had more fun.

# THE EXPLORER

**Skateboarders love to skate spots that the Norms completely ignore, to reappropriate the bland features of the cityscape and all that. For some, it can become an obsession.**

If you skateboard long enough, you're going to start looking at the world from a funny perspective: trash cans become obstacles to jump over; planters, curbs, and benches become ledges to grind and slide; angled walls, railings, and smooth concrete begin to take on the status of holy grails. If you're lucky enough to find yourself skating one of these hallowed grounds, you are probably going to get so excited that you have to tell all your friends about it. Imagine if you found this place, called your mates to share your discovery, then went back only to find it has been ABD'd (that's "already been done" for all you Norms out there) to death or, even worse, that it's been knobbed by killjoy city workers and has joined the list of great skate spots in the sky.

In the event of uncovering a previously undiscovered spot, the trick is to keep this knowledge to yourself until the time is right. This might be when you're out skating with a bunch of guys you know won't want to session the spot anyway, giving you the perfect opportunity to show off. It also could be when that famous pro skater is in town on tour—they'll probably think you're cool for giving up such an amazing spot—or that day when you wake up and you just know it's the right time to go. Having said that, if you stand back and think about it, does it really matter when you return? After all, unless you're deep in the industry, the fact tricks are ABD doesn't matter one little bit. And let's be honest, if you are in the skate trade, you ain't out finding spots, your filmer and photographers can do all that hard work for you.

I mean, one way to secure the spot's virginity would be to, say, use a bike lock or similar to block the spot. This ensures YOU (you asshole!) are the only one with a key, only YOU can skate it, only when YOU want, and only with who YOU choose. Be warned, if you ever want to be liked by anyone ever again, dismiss this idea immediately. Instead, enjoy the good times you're going to have skating that new cellar door, quirky rail, or perfect kicker, because nothing lasts forever. Simply skate it while you can and don't take it too seriously.

In summary, the rules are fairly simple (sort of!): search for new stuff all the time, enjoy being (possibly) the first person to skate a new spot, but don't be a ballbag worrying about who's going to do what trick on "your" spot or who/what may have come before or after you. It doesn't matter. Enjoy it, share it, and don't be an asshole. Simple.

# THE SHOP OWNER

**In skateboarding, people talk a lot about "doing it for the love," but these guys are the real deal. Shop Owners live on the brink of bankruptcy just to make sure you have somewhere to buy your skate stuff. Where would we be without them?**

I'm not talking about the chain "skate store" at the local mall or the free-delivery-on-orders-over-X-amount-dot-com e-shacks. I'm talking about skate shops—the real down-to-earth hubs of skate life.

In the days prior to the Internet, kids, you had to leave your bedroom if you wanted to go and buy something. We had "cash"—paper and metal icons that represented money—that you used to put in the hand of a human at a specific location in exchange for the objects you required or desired. It was a fairly ubiquitous process, until people decided that those pesky overheads like electricity, rent, and employees should be circumnavigated to make it all more cost effective (read bland).

Before the days when video parts were just a footnote on your Facebook feed, they used to be sold on magnetic tapes and laser discs in bespoke emporiums known as "skate shops." These curious places stocked other things, too: skateboard decks, skateboard shoes, stickers, and other associated paraphernalia. When you walked into one, you would be amazed by the stale smell engrained in the fabric of the shop after years of young skate-rat employees eating bad food. Visitors were wowed by racks of boards with crazy bizarre graphics and confused by the strange conversations about the video that was playing on loop. These places made you feel like a strange visitor to a new world, until you realized that these people were your people. The Shop Owners would take you under their wing, teach you to respect skateboarding, and make sure you had enough common sense to make your way in the world. Occasionally they might make fun of you, but they could also make you feel special by offering you a free sticker or allowing you to use the cramped shop toilet instead of finding some nearby fast-food joint to drop your load. These places, the owners, and sometimes even the customers were—and in a few small niches still are—like big brothers teaching the ways of skateboarding, bringing you up right, and learning you some respect.

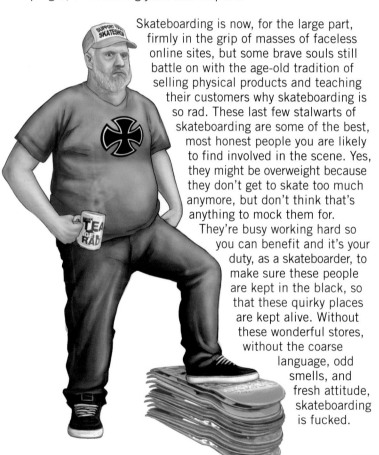

Skateboarding is now, for the large part, firmly in the grip of masses of faceless online sites, but some brave souls still battle on with the age-old tradition of selling physical products and teaching their customers why skateboarding is so rad. These last few stalwarts of skateboarding are some of the best, most honest people you are likely to find involved in the scene. Yes, they might be overweight because they don't get to skate too much anymore, but don't think that's anything to mock them for. They're busy working hard so you can benefit and it's your duty, as a skateboarder, to make sure these people are kept in the black, so that these quirky places are kept alive. Without these wonderful stores, without the coarse language, odd smells, and fresh attitude, skateboarding is fucked.

# THE HISTORIAN

**Armed with a disposable income from his nine-to-five and a vested interest in skateboarding's past, the Historian keeps obscure skateboard graphics highly priced and extremely sought after.**

You know when you go into one of those sports bars or old pubs, the ones with all that useless crap on the walls, and you wonder where they found all this weird stuff? Well, the answer is probably the Internet, but ignore that. What I'm getting at is that chances are even the most determined bar owner doesn't have just a drop of the dedication a true skateboard historian displays.

This guy is not interested in the reissued boards that companies seem all too happy to churn out these days. He wants the original deck—the one with the legacy, the meaning, and the value that is connected with the OG deal. All that comes at a cost.

Your average skater might, at some point in later life, find himself absentmindedly searching forums and eBay to see if anyone is selling the first

board he ever rode. To own again the deck and graphic that kickstarted a life-long passion is understandable—a reminder of the good old days—but the difference between this older you and the Historian is that he will not stop at just one or two boards. The real Historian is an obsessive. It starts slowly, sure, but before long it's all he does, all he thinks about, all he talks about.

The first sign you're a budding Historian is when you realize there's not enough wall space left to hang all the decks you've amassed. Instead, you're buying boards to look at just once before packing them up and stashing them away in a cupboard. Soon, any Historian worth his salt is going to fill the house, the shed, and then the garage with as many decks and other bits of skateboard history as he can get his hands on. Eventually, it could be enough to fill a small museum, because with each piece of memorabilia gathered comes a story—the story of its place in skateboarding's past. The Historian knows all these anecdotes and he'll happily bore you with them... Maybe a museum's not such a bad idea...

After amassing such a vast collection, it's more than likely the Historian's wife is seriously considering leaving him, because his collectibles are all he'll talk about. What happened to that creative, healthy young man she married? Now he's a skate nerd, there's no room left anywhere in the house, and the bank balance is taking a pounding, all because of a few stupid planks of wood. He's like a damn stamp collector who spends hours searching eBay for pointless things to spend cash on, or one of those guys who buys Star Wars toys and never unwraps them for fear of losing value. It's now gotten to the point where he's spending more time trawling the Internet looking for that OG Randy Colvin deck (with the black bag) than he is actually going skateboarding. All is lost!

The Historian will not find it easy to hear the warnings of his other half, or any other rational person for that matter. He's in control, don't worry about it. "It's not an obsession, it's just a bit of fun, what's the harm? And, to be honest, if anything, it's an investment," he tells himself as his wife slams the door on the way. "Shit, she's taken the kids. Oh well, that's more space for the collection!" He gleefully thinks to himself.

# THE LOCAL

**Like a snarling dog parading back and forth behind a fence, the Local wants you to know that this is his turf and he'll puff out his chest to make sure you are in no doubt about who's in charge.**

There are a few tell-tale signs that you have this variety of skateboarder in your presence and, once you know what to look for, Locals can be easy to spot. The first thing to do is simply use your eyes.

Graffiti is by far the clearest sign that lets you know you're dealing with one of these characters. In this situation, the writing is quite literally on the wall. Or the floor. Or both. The crudely scrawled mantras of "Locals Only" and "Posers Go Home" make their point fairly clear, but often you can find them embellished with a skull and crossbones, pentagrams, or swastikas—anything offensive really—just for good measure.

This hangover from the attitude-filled 80s is generally aimed at the Norms, telling the suits in no uncertain terms to stay away. But if you're a little on the timid side you might be put off, even if you skate yourself. Here, the main thing to note is that most of the time this anti-social act of bravado is purely for show. Beneath the thin veneer of intimidation is a complex mix of a desire to be noticed and a never-been-loved cry for help. In other words, a tear jerker of a story waiting to be told.

Of course, it could also be that the guy who wrote this stuff is genuinely a bit unhinged. In which case, I'd advise you to use your judgment and either ingratiate yourself with the Local by buying him a case of beer or otherwise be prepared to high tail it out of there the moment you think that he's taking exception to you criddling on his patch.

Provided you survived this frosty encounter with an unhinged Local, it might do you well to prepare yourself for the second, less-obvious version of the species. This example can be spotted at skateparks and skate spots the world over, and, to be honest, the likelihood of you finding him or her before they find you is a task not worth undertaking. In their heads they run this place, and you're a new kid on their turf and they know it, so they are going try and push your buttons.

Efforts to antagonize could be something as harmless as a mean mugging— a stink-eye from across the park or a shoulder barge as a Local skates past you. It also could be something more verbal: a muttered curse under the breath, perhaps. Whatever form it takes, this jockish behavior should be disregarded. Leave karma to sort out this kind of idiotic bullshit—impotence, public humiliation, or simply a bone-crunching slam should usually balance the books.

Regardless of whether you're on the receiving end of a cold shoulder or a jock bullying technique, the main thing to remember is just to ignore that shit—they're the idiots. You're out there trying to get yours and that's the most important thing. If some ignorant fool thinks you need to pay the toll to pass this bridge, then they're the real losers.

# THE ENGINEER

**For some, geekery is a way of life. To them it's inconceivable that everyone else doesn't think in algorithms and calculus. These are the Engineers.**

No matter what the "sport" or discipline, there are always those who find pleasure in the activity from different angles to the masses, aware their talents lie in other areas. Compare the referee to the player, the gambler to the jockey—these guys know it all, they love it, but they are happy not to be the ones getting involved. In skating, there are no rules and no form to worry about, so people manifest their interest in other ways.

Being a skateboarding geek can mean more than knowing the name of every trick, who did what at that spot, or who skated to what song in that video. True geekery means number crunching and analyzing. From studying the chemical formulas of polyurethane wheels to the angles used in ramp construction, the science is there if you want to pay attention to it.

In the innocent past, it was normal to find people trying to soften bushings by boiling them in Ma's best pan, or spending Sundays figuring out how to build jump ramps. During the small-wheel craze of the early 90s, skaters clamped their "oversized" wheels to the lathe in woodwork class and shaved them down to within a few millimeters of the bearings. Although commendable, technically these attempts are amateur. Geekery has way more to offer.

Some people (true geeks) take the urge to innovate to the next level, making it their life's work to figure out the best, most efficient ways to create ever "better" boards, wheels, and ramps. You only have to visit one of the industry trade shows to get an up-to-date list of things not to bother looking for in your local skate shop: square wheels, fabric grip tape, under-board lighting kits like the ones jocks have on their cars. The list of people hell-bent on reinventing the wheel is quite astounding. For the most part though, these Willy-Wonka types are met with a flat response from the skate community, a group notorious for regarding change as unnecessary. When the Engineer showcases his latest fiberglass composite board to skaters, he's usually met with indifference at best.

Of course, not every innovator can be chastized as useless, but a quick look at the successful reinventions of the last few decades shows you how elite this group is. I think the last officially accepted invention that didn't go the way of the dodo was the double kick tail. That was about 20 years ago and now, again, people are into riding old designs that predate the modern shape. If anything, skateboarding is regressing. As a result, if you're a budding nerd with a burning desire to change skating, you're going to find it hard to make things work, let alone make ends meet trying to peddle your wares, so my advice would be: don't bother. Even if you do create the unbreakable board, the never diminishing wheel, or the unscrapable shoe, your business model is going to be flawed as no one will ever need a second one/pair.

Back to the drawing board.

# PENNYBOARDER

**Not content to skate the perfectly suitable, proven, and functional seven-ply maple skateboard we're all familiar with these days, the Pennyboarder is that rare breed of tweaker who prefers to own a plastic board just like the one your dad (or maybe even granddad) rode in the 70s.**

"Why?" I hear you ask, and I'm not sure I have a satisfactory answer for you. To be honest, I don't get 'em, but I'm willing to have a guess at why these retro-obsessed morons own these ridiculous things.

One tack of reasoning I have developed is that maybe, like everyone else in the world at the moment, these people are looking back at the past and realizing how cool it all seemed: the hair, the gaudy colors, the high rates of unemployment...

Everyone—from those hipsters wearing donkey jackets that make you look like a 1950s removal man (but one with shorter jeans and more asymmetric hair) to the guy in the vintage apron with the waxed mustache selling traditionally prepared spelt loaves from his over-priced yet well-tiled minimalist artisan food emporium—owns things like Pennyboards. They're happy to add another retro element to their life, no matter how anachronistic it may be to mix up the decades. It's a strange person who looks back at the past as a time when things were "better," when they've only been on this earth for 20 short years themselves.

Another possible reason that everyone loves these abominations to the spirit of skateboarding is that Pennyboards are just SO damn cute! Looking at the range of colors is more like opening a bag of jelly beans than flicking through a skateboard catalog, which means tight-T-shirted guys and powder-puff high-school girls can happily match their boards to their heinous outfits.

If you're going to go down this route you might as well get one for each day of the week—just don't forget to pick out a matching outfit for your annoying little dog, too!

Whatever the thought process behind buying one of these neon atrocities, you can be sure that everybody who owns a Pennyboard has difficulty not looking like a total novice when riding the thing. You can easily tell when one is coming your way, because people trying to control the board will have their arms stuck straight out in a quarter-to-three position, as they desperately attempt to stop themselves from plowing their little fluorescent dart into innocent passers by. The head of the out-of-control rider will be bobbing side to side in sympathy with the flailing arms, while the feet will be set firmly in a fencing stance thanks to inexperience and the fact the boards are barely wide enough to accommodate a size six flip-flop. This is never a good look, so the sooner you take that plastic eyesore and leave it in your garage to collect dust, the better.

# WHEELBITER

**This guy is everywhere these days. With him it's a clear-cut case of fashion over function—the kid just ain't in it for the long haul.**

There are always going to be those people who can't quite figure out who it is they are, where they want to be in life, or what the hell they're into. This kind of person has no option but to be a follower; someone who is led blindly like a myopic sheep; that guy who likes whatever he's told to like and thinks however the media tell him to think. He's the dude with the shiny new skateboard who approaches you randomly in the street, hoping to find a kindred spirit and someone to share his new interest with. Chances are he'll be wearing some over-logoed, surf-company T-shirt, with too much product in his hair and strangely spotless sneakers. In cases where this guy is a bit more incognito, you might identify him by the lack of scratches on his brand-new setup or the flailing arms as he tries desperately to tame that awkward plank of wood beneath his feet.

If he's a young guy, he probably got this great idea from some men's fashion magazine. A hot new trend has been spotted and he's read the article explaining how to pull off being a "skater," what brands are cool, and the required terminology needed to get you in the club. This advice is, of course, one hundred percent pure, fresh, and steaming horseshit. If you think you're going to get accepted in this already exclusive club, you're going to have to show a little more commitment than that.

In the less likely eventuality he's over 30, you can bet your life he's going to be claiming he used to skate back in the day. Now, having read this piece in that men's magazine he subscribes to (the "arty" one his wife won't think he's a pervert for having), he's convinced skating is how to regain his youth and some much-needed cool points. In an effort to win you over, he'll name-drop some of the more obvious 80s superstars and reference things like Kryptonics wheels, despite the fact you probably weren't born yet when they stopped being produced.

Either way, young or old, these efforts will sadly be in vain, because real skaters know that skateboarding is for life, not just for Christmas. No matter how well these Wheelbiters think they are doing, in the heads of all the lifers, they are part-timers, kooks, marks, and try-hards—that's a hard thing to overlook.

Therefore, my advice to any journalist commissioned to write a "How to Be a Skater" article in any future magazines is to dish out this simple, realistic nugget of knowledge to your readers (provided by me, to you, free of charge):

"Get a board, go out, and take a slam, then get up and take another."

See, if you take a slam and get up and try again, it means you're really trying, and that's how to be a skater.

# THE BRAT

**Highly strung way beyond his years, used to getting his own way, and very hard to like, the Brat is everyone's least favorite person to be around, especially if you're broke.**

When you're a kid growing up, maybe you don't notice the financial divides or parenting differences that exist between the families of you and your friends. When the boy down the street has all the newest toys, you just want to go and play with him. You might not like the kid, he might treat you like an idiot, but that doesn't matter—you just want to get your hands on those cool toys, that's all. And when the guy up the street is given a skateboard and you are desperate to try skateboarding, it's going to make it even more difficult to resist the temptation to hang out with him.

As you get older, you might begin to realize that a Brat who has all the new stuff, all of the time, isn't quite as much fun to be around as you thought. He never takes his own lunches to school and he makes fun of you because you have to. He doesn't have birthday parties at home, he goes to the fancy pizza place with all the arcade games and the animatronic band of animals who perform songs. He doesn't have to eat whatever his parents put on his plate, he cries until he gets his way. The Brat doesn't value anything and you're slowly beginning to realize that he's actually a bit of a dick. He's a whiner, he's a little bitch... What a pain in the ass.

Well, that was when you were young; now he's older and you've both stuck with skateboarding. Unsurprisingly, he's got all the new shit as soon as it comes out, just as he always has done. His shoes will always be scuff-free, because scuffs mean they're old and that means it's time for a new pair. When that new board's got a ding in it, he demands another from his mother, who immediately supplies him with a fresh one straight off the rack. It had better be the right brand, or mom's going to have to go right back to the skate shop and pick up the correct one. While you're scraping together pocket money and saving up your birthday gifts to get enough cash together for a new deck, this guy's flying through them at a rate of knots. It sucks, but shit happens. Is he still whining about his life?

Luckily, it's not all bad news. If you know one of these guys, all you've got to do is learn to be around when he loses interest in the board he's riding or decides he's over his current sneakers. Accepting his cast-offs is a humble position to be in, but at least it means you can skate, right? You'd just better hope you can get to his board before he has a tantrum and puts a foot through the wood. And pray you both share the same shoe size, otherwise you'd better learn to put up with squeezing into his hand-me-downs.

When it gets to the point where you can't stand getting this dude's cast offs any longer, you can always take solace in the knowledge that this guy's never going to truly enjoy himself, appreciate what he's got, or like what he's going to get next, because it all has no worth to him. This makes you the better person; enjoy that.

# THE FAN

**Screaming, whooping, hollering, and full to the brim with energy drinks, the Fan—with his bloodstream dangerously full of sugar—takes all skateboarding contests very seriously.**

The training-hard-for-the-win, trophy-hunting, and glory-seeking ideologies present in most mainstream sports do not factor heavily in most skateboarders' vision of what true skateboarding is. However, like it or not, competitions do exist and to some riders they are a huge deal, and the same thing goes for some fans. It is specifically the emergence of this fervent follower of competitive skateboarding that truly indicates a departure from the "sport's" lackadaisical approach to the competitions of yesteryear. The once industry-only, laissez-faire attitude to contests, where no one really cared who won or lost, has been pushed aside to make way for a new, big-money, high-stakes modern incarnation. This version is now way too lucrative for skateboarding—and those within the scene to whom winning actually means something—not to take notice.

It's not just the format and statistical nature of these events that can force a yawn; it's also the fact that the only riders invited are the ones able repeatedly to perform trick after eye-melting trick while under the extreme pressure created by a first prize of a quarter of a million notes. In this environment, the creative side of skateboarding is unsurprisingly less important and therefore less represented. It seems the more money you throw at these endeavors, the more mind numbing they are to watch, and it's the lo-fi, counter-culture, rough-around-the-edges events that always make for more exciting footage. But that's just my opinion, man.

The Fan doesn't care about this, instead he laps it up. He doesn't mind the expensive tickets, the long lines for the bathroom, or the over-priced food. The bland sterility created by modern, statistics-led score-keeping enraptures the Fan's sensibilities, because now he can figure out who's winning— and it's all about winning, not taking part. With big money on the line, the serious-o-meter is permanently ramped up to 11— all those close-up, slo-mo replays of riders' anguish-filled faces as they start their final attempts confirm this shit is serious.

So where did these Fans come from? They're usually the ones were never good at skating, or who didn't see the point in sticking with it when they can just turn up at the stadium in their fresh duds and feel like they're still a part of it all.

This unathletic approach to an energetic pastime has obvious downsides. The amount of time spent sitting, watching, instead of actually doing, the activity he enjoys has undoubtedly given him a more plump physique, and maybe the beginnings of Type 2 diabetes. The gigantic buckets of soda and plentiful array of artery-clogging snacks offered at the food stands aren't helping the waistband, but the Fan does get some exercise: screaming his head off and punching the air along with the winner, who has just bagged enough cash to get that diamond-encrusted Rolex he's always wanted. Mo' money, mo' problems.

As the victor takes to the podium, the stadium is filled with the cheers of the crowd and emotions reach fever pitch, right until the point when the organizers kick everyone out because the show's over. Nobody's grabbing their board to go skate once the ceremony is done; they just go home. Meanwhile, back at the arena, ramp builders shuffle in to tear down this perfect skatepark and clean the sticky bleacher floors before the fair moves on to the next town.

# SECURITY GUARD

## While you just want to express yourself through the medium of skateboarding, some people want to stop you at all costs. Meet the Security Guard.

Rent-a-cops, which these guys are frequently called, are the number one pain in the ass of every street skater the world over. Their "official" position and police-style uniforms mean that the one generalization most of us are guaranteed to make about these guys is that they were obviously just too fat and lazy to get jobs as real cops. While this may be true of a fair number, there are exceptions to the rule. To make this task a little less all encompassing, I'll split these characters into two categories: C**ts & Grunts.

The first example unfortunately makes up the majority of the guys walking the beat. These are the men who have dreamed about being a cop ever since they were a kid. Life on the force was all they ever wanted, their dream, but thanks to failing eyesight, lack of physical prowess at cop school, or a questionable mental state, they just didn't cut the mustard. After their applications were denied, their dreams were left crushed as they realized they were destined never to don the blue uniform and defend the world from evil. The trouble is that with this inability to fulfill their dreams, failed policemen have become enraged, bitter, and unreasonable, but they seem to have found the next best outlet for their power-trip dream: security.

You will know if you have encountered one such Security Guard when you see him running at you from across the parking lot, calling for backup without even first engaging you in adult conversation. These guys are in many ways worse than regular cops because they have all of the desire to fight "crime," but none of the training required to carry out the task correctly.

The techniques may vary from country to country and from business to business, but when someone employed by a fast-food joint starts coming in hot, like one of the president's men, you're in for a treat. This guy has been waiting all day to spring into action and he's not going to let you go until the boys in blue show up. His oversized gut should make sure you can't escape and while being tackled to the ground and restrained may be fun for the guard, it doesn't bode well for your body or your rap sheet.

Of course, this is only one type of asshole, and there are others who opt for a less asshole-ish approach while still trying to kick you out of a spot... The assholes! These are the aforementioned grunts; the guys out there just doing a job. They didn't score an F at cop school or dream of one day being in charge of a sidearm, these guys only want to make their day's wage and be done with it. To them, security work is a job, end of—no different from working the checkout counter at the grocery. It's not their office block, car park, or handrail you are skating, they're just being paid to kick you off it. This is the kind of guy you can often reason with. Try something like this if you want to attempt to hang around there for longer: *assuming an innocent voice and smiling* "Oh really, we're not allowed to skate here? Well, we're not causing anyone any harm and we'll be gone in five minutes..." Here, the main thing to remember is you're going to get more playtime if you're nice to them, so it really can pay to be polite.

# THE ENEMIES

**Being a skateboarder gives you the unwavering right to act like you are better than any of the other "user groups" that populate street spots and skate parks. It's all about a lofty sense of self-importance and knowing that your discipline really is better than everyone else's. It's your prerogative.**

The Man thinks we are all part of the same "x-treme" family, that we all hang out together, talking about what tricks are cool and how we all get along in some weird action-sports pact. It's not like that at all. There is a pecking order, an unspoken directory of acceptability and credibility, and it is crucial you understand it so you can inform Norms this is not a "we're all in it together" type of deal. It's is a war of attrition. Don't forget other users are not our friends. You must know your enemy! The pros and cons of these enemies are detailed below.

### The BMXer
Our two-wheeled brethren are by far the most accepted subsection of the extreme but they are far from your friend and here are a few reasons why you might want to shoot a few moody sideways glances at them when they roll up to your session.

### Cons:
• The thing they ride is a gigantic piece of metal, so if they're coming at you out of control, it's going to hurt.
• They go faster than all the rest of your enemies, which combined with the last point means more pain at a faster rate.
• They will always beat you in a fight, as 95% of their muscle mass is located in their deformed upper body.
• They all think they're Sid Vicious or something.

• These days it's cool not to use brakes. What. The. Hell. No Brakes. No Brains!
• Their pegs ruin our ledges when they grind them.
• Their asses permanently stick out of their jeans. When pedalling their boxers hang out like a baboon's flappy, red-skinned ass.
**Pros**:
• They wear skate shoes, keeping skate-shoe companies in business.

## The Rollerblader

Ah, the fruitbooter. We're not talking about beach boulevard cruising, bikini-clad, well-toned, MILFs here. We're talking about dudes who do it in the streets, man. Last time I checked, they called themselves "aggressive in-liners" after they'd realized they couldn't use the term "skater." You might know them better as "bin liners," and if it wasn't for the passing of time, they would be way lower down the list. Thanks to changing times, these rare beasts are almost completely extinct, which kind of makes them oddly more acceptable, but they still suck. And here are a few reasons why...

**Cons:**
• They used to wear the baggiest clothes imaginable and now they dress like metro-sexuals. The baggy faze was dumb, but it was way more legit than this new shit they've got going on.
• They wax everything. I mean everything. Even the floor. What is that about!?
• Some of them step into instead of jump onto their grinds, seriously, they are attached to you feet, how hard can it be?
• They have no friends left who Rollerblade because everyone else stopped doing it 10 years ago, so they have to put their headphones in for company, which means they don't pay attention and always get in your way.
• They don't understand how dumb they look when they go Rollerblading, which means they don't understand that you hate them. This is just somehow annoying.
• Did I mention that they wax everything?
**Pros:**
• It's fun to watch them try to walk up stairs.

## The Rollerbooter

There is a clear distinction to make here between those who ride quads (rollerbooters) and those who ride "inlines."

**Cons:**
• When the disco beats from their boombox get them all juiced, they start pulling some really weird dance moves. Very off-putting. If no boombox is present, they always have headphones on and are completely oblivious to their surroundings.
• They wear leg warmers.
• When skating backward, they wiggle their hips from side to side while looking over their shoulders. When they come toward you, it's like they're trying to hypnotize you with their ass. Creepy.

**Pros:**
• It's funny when you see them skate ramps sideways with their feet pointing in opposite directions.

## The Longboarder

I wrote an entry on these guys (see page 20) featuring a whole load of cons and I'm struggling to think of the pros... OK here are two: they help keep skater-owned shops in the black, and they might have a skate tool you could borrow when in a tight spot. Is it even the same mounting hardware they use? I hate them so much I don't even want to find out.

## The Free Runner

This "action sport" is basically an extension of that childhood desire to run around, jumping off stuff, except no one bothered to tell these guys they're actually old enough to start doing something a bit less shit. In their heads, they're performing the intro to a James Bond sequel, in reality they're leap-frogging trash cans and trying to pass off falling over as style.

**Cons:**
• When one of them breaks his or her neck trying to jump off that building next to the skatepark, the Man shuts down the park because in his eyes you're all part of the same "sport."
• In the future these guys will probably get paid loads of cash for being in James Bond film intros.

• Even if they fail miserably to perform their "tricks," they'll still be an Internet sensation because their falls are some of the worst you're likely to see.
**Pros:**
• There are about ten of them in the world, so it's not really a huge problem.

## The Scooter Kid

A serious issue in parts of Europe; the UK is crawling with them, for instance. That's where I'm from, so these guys are the worst of the worst as far as I'm concerned. I'm not talking about a small problem, it's like a plague of locusts, ignorant, pre-pubescent, idiot locusts. On shiny metal wheels. Where to begin...

**Cons:**
• They are clueless when it comes to skatepark etiquette. I mean, it's an unwritten list of rules but it's not hard to learn them. Unless you're a scooter moron.
• They do that diving-board thing, where they half hang a scooter over the coping so they're in the way even before they're riding the ramp.
• They don't really bother landing tricks. How it can be OK to "fake make" a trick when you're standing on and holding onto your equipment is beyond me.
• One of their "tricks" involves spinning the scooter around their head without checking who's behind them, which is similar to a ninja coming at you with nunchucks when you least expect it. Except it's not as cool as a ninja.
• They're so young that when they eventually cause you to crash into them, their parents think it's your fault and want to fight or sue you.
• They are all out of their faces on energy drinks and their parents leave them out to play all day, as though the skatepark is a daycare center.
**Pros:**
The videos on them eating shit on YouTube are roll-on-the-floor-laughing funny.

# THE MYTH

**Sasquatch, leprechauns, unicorns, the Loch Ness Monster, a world free from kids on scooters... all these things share one glaringly obvious trait: they don't exist. The Myth is a bit more of a gray area. He is definitely a real person, because your friend's friend once met him and that friend knows this one thing the Myth did must be true because his friend said so. Make sense? Good.**

Every town and every city has one local skateboarder who has achieved mythical status through his skateboarding.

"I heard he did this insane trick at the spot."

"No way man, I heard he did it switch."

"I heard he did it after being hit by a car."

"I heard he did it naked!"

Mixing the Chinese-whisper effect that younger skateboarders create during their junk-food fueled conversations with the murky, beer-fueled memories of the reminiscing older generation easily can create a make-believe memory of a skateboarder, one that can be at least 50 percent fiction. The person may have existed, but exactly what he did or didn't do may have been somewhat altered.

Usually this mythical beast will have dropped off the scene due to some career-shortening, never-heard-of-before injury, or he simply disappeared into the ether after allegedly doing some mind-bending super stunt. This kind of exit from the skateboard game means this ethereal creature's spirit is destined to live on in infamy. The drab reality is that this apparition, this distant memory probably just got older and had to join the rat-race and accept the responsibilities of real life. He probably had a kid, got a 9-5, and just ended up skating less.

Regardless of the actual truth behind the stories, the enhancing of the Myth's abilities, and truth-bending surrounding his stunt work, this guy is probably the most important person to figure in the formation of a young skater's life. The mysteries and fables only serve to make a kid aspirational about what is possible on a skateboard. Without these fantastical stories, kids might think some things are just not humanly possible, and one of the most amazing things about skateboarding is how it continues to progress beyond what seemed possible in the years preceeding it. Without knowing it, the Myth is the person we learn from, the one who teaches us lessons, inspires us, and makes us believe the impossible is possible. The Myth might not know it, but he is.

Next time someone tells you a tale about the time the local legend did such and such, don't question it and wonder about the validity of the statement; embellish it and relay it to someone else. It's the only way to ensure things move forward. And it's fun to fuck with people's heads, too.

# THE STRESSER

**It's a fact that the majority of skateboarders on this planet are teenage boys, and if there's one thing teenage boys have, it's plenty of angst. The hormonal changes brought about by the aging process mean boys express new feelings, many of which often aren't pleasant to be around.**

Snapping boards, shouting at handrails, ripping off T-shirts are all classic signs that the scarlet-faced person in front of you is a Stresser. But what causes a Stresser to be so stressed? Surely skateboarding is a release, something that takes your mind off all the things that make you angry. Well, not for everyone. To some people, skateboarding is the single most frustrating act they can undertake.

The crack in the ground that the skater spies just as he's about to attempt a trick manifests itself as an impossible-to-overcome chasm across his path, one he just can't get out of his mind. The barking dog from across the parking lot becomes a distraction of massive proportions. Cars parked in the landing area, cars parked in the run up, a rail made from the wrong kind of metal, gum on grip tape, or simply not being able to skate away after having made a trick can all make the majority of us a bit pissed, but the Stresser always goes one step further.

These angry young men possess hair-trigger reactions that can result in the most out-of-proportion responses to the most inconsequential of problems. Think of the small amount of bad luck needed to hit a stone while skating. Now imagine hitting that stone and pulverizing your skateboard to such an extent that you have to fork out your hard-earned cash to buy a new one. This kind of over-the-top response might seem like a good idea at the time, but it rarely is.

There is a degree of acceptance of this mad behavior that exists within skateboarding. In special circumstances, it can even help make someone's career—such hockey-tempered skaters otherwise might have faded into obscurity years earlier had they managed to keep their cool. To the person on the outside of the madness looking in, these outbursts are hilarious. Occasionally, it can be scary to see someone lose his mind but, in retrospect, it's always funny. If a skater is foolish enough to throw a tantrum while being filmed by his friend, then he is far more likely to be remembered for that eruption than any landed trick he might have been fortunate enough to put down that day.

Often there is the added disgrace of having to perform the "Walk of Shame" (aka the act of skulking away to pick up your board after throwing it away in a particularly dumb fit of rage). Equally embarrassing is the ankle tweak that you gave yourself after failing to focus (see page 110) your board correctly, as is the visit to the hospital for the broken hand you achieved after punching your deck in anger.

All of these outbursts may seem trivial, comical even, but I think they can be blamed on a large amount of OCD in the skateboard community. Forcing the mind to focus on repetitive checks and ticks, rather than concentrating on all the randomness and bad luck of the real world, drives many skaters slowly insane. So if you want to avoid becoming the kind of guy who has to turn his light switch off and on 20 times before leaving the house, maybe you should think about growing up and chilling out a bit. Or perhaps just consider setting yourself more attainable goals and trying to be happy with what you've got. Life's too short.

# RAMP BUILDER

**Since the first skater realized the benefits of riding up curves, the race was on to figure out how it could be done more and more regularly, and closer and closer to home. Enter, the Ramp Builder.**

The backyard ramp can vary from an asymmetric, piecemeal mish-mash of stolen wood built by teenagers to a precision-engineered ramp constructed by some kid's dad who can draw up a set of blueprints and knows his way around a circular saw. Whatever the result, a ramp in your backyard is pretty much every kid's dream and, to be honest, it's the dream of most adult skaters, too.

Much more than a mere training facility for the skater of the house, the home ramp offers an instant session at any time of the day or night he might choose. The design can be as unchanging or as variable as a skater might like. It can be chopped and changed at his discretion, ripped apart and rebuilt however he fancies. Sadly, for most of us, a ramp outside the bedroom window remains a fantasy. There are restrictions and problems that'll rear their heads from every angle imaginable—from the space available to parental permission and grumpy neighbors. Turning a ramp dream into reality is a tough one to pull off.

Still, there are those prepared to give building a ramp a shot. So, provided you've got the ability to erect one, what do you need to know about the backyard ramp? Here's a cheat sheet in case you're thinking about joining the ranks of rad.

## The Build

Unless you're loaded, you're going to be making this yourself and you're going to need some sort of a plan. The wood can be scavenged, stolen, borrowed, or even paid for, but it takes a load of lumber to make a ramp happen. I'm sure you can get some ramp designs from the Internet, but you're going to need tools and someone who vaguely knows what they're doing. If you don't know what coping you want, what transition to use, or what wood works best on the surface, then find out—or make it up, it's your ramp after all.

## The Sessions

Now that you have your own personal halfpipe, you will be inundated with more friends than you ever knew you had. The trouble is now you must decide which mates you're going to reveal the exact location of the ramp to and which "friends" you are going to fob off with vague directions to where it is. It's best to keep it tight if you're worried about the next-door neighbors, your parents, or, indeed, you being annoyed by a sudden influx of skaters.

## Maintenance

After a while, this thing is going to get holes in it—the coping's going to rust, and the wood's going to rot, so you'd better be prepared to spend some time looking after all your hard work. The question is: who's going to pay for it when things go wrong?

## The Ramp Jam

The fact you can have your friends around for a skate at any time means that, once you're old enough, you can start adding loud music, members of the opposite sex, and beer into the mix. This is when things get really interesting. In fact, this is a good opportunity to get some donations for more wood, maybe you should set the party up as a fundraiser.

# THE SKATE HOUSE

**If you're the kind of dedicated skateboarder who doesn't throw in the towel at the first sign of interest from the opposite sex, external pressures from real life, or the belief that you need to "grow up," then you are well on your way to being considered a lifer. At some point, provided you've sidestepped all the previously mentioned crap trying to force itself on you, you're probably going to find yourself living with other skateboarders, and, unless you're fortunate enough to be rolling in cash, it's going to be a bit of a shithole. In case you're not prepared for what to expect, here's a list of things to be aware of.**

## The Location

Let's face it, you and your friends aren't going to be living in a penthouse or beachfront pad, so it might serve you well to set your sights low. Primarily, it should be near a good spot to skate, that way you're always going to be able to shred. Finding a house that is somewhere not in gang-banger territory would be a safer option. One way to get somewhere in a nicer part of town is to lie your ass off when dealing with potential landlords. People have their preconceptions about skaters, so for the record, you don't smoke, there are only three of you living there, you all have steady jobs, and you probably do something other than skateboard in your spare time, like Frisbee.

## The Housemates

This element is up to you. If you're sharing with friends, be prepared for the risk that you might not be buds anymore by the end of the rental period. He might be your best buddy on a board, but when he owes you rent, eats all your food, and sub-lets his room out to a toothless punk to grow weed in, you might be forgiven for changing your mind about him and re-evaluating your friendship. Having a mix of boys and girls might be a rough ride—there will be an inevitable hook up and bad breakup situation—but it's going to be no worse than living in a same-sex environment. The most important thing is to find people who are honest above all else.

### The Smell

When you start sharing with a large number of skaters, one of the first things you're going to notice is that at least 50 percent of skateboarders' feet stink. This stench, combined with the lack of laundry that's being done (unless everyone's mom still does it—but seriously, come on, how old are you guys?) and the constant reek of cigarette smoke and farts, is going to be strong, so you might want to invest in some air fresheners, incense burners, josticks, or something else to stop you gagging.

### The Diet

As you're fresh outta your parents' house, you're probably going to be slightly lacking in the culinary department. You need to be prepared for a diet that consists of two meals: pasta with sauce and pizza. You'll fast realize that pasta is good for maximum input of carbs at minimum cost. Pizza is the lazy option and has the benefit that you will have something for breakfast tomorrow, provided you haven't got an entourage of famished friends around, eyeing up your leftovers.

Do you like the way your heart beats? If so, it might be worth doing your body a solid favor and buying a lettuce once a month or something.

## The Parties

P-A-R-T-Why? Because you guys have moved out of your parents' spare rooms! You don't really need a reason to have a party, and you'll find the mere fact you have an apartment and you know skateboarders is enough of an excuse to throw one. We're not talking kegs of beer and toga parties here, we're talking rooms crammed with people drinking the cheapest beer and smoking the piffest weed they can find. With any luck, you'll be able to live off your guests' spare beers and they won't get so wild that you're going to lose your deposit.

## The Couch

So, I hope last night was good fun, but it's the morning after and your hangover requires a little mindless TV. Time to wake up that random body on the couch. Again.

One thing you'll find, party or no party, is that your couch is going to double up as a spare, rent-free bed for a continuous rotation of friends, international visitors, and party casualties. My advice is don't be shy, wake 'em up, and make them get the coffee on.

## The Bathroom

This place is going to be a shock. An apartment full of beer-swilling idiots combined with the first-time-away-from-home cleaning habits of your fellow rent payers doesn't make for a nice place to have a shower. Think skid marks, stink, hair in the drain, and mold. If you're not holding your nose and wearing flip flops in the shower within a month or two, you're very brave.

# THE ALKY

**Skateboarding seems always to have had a relationship with booze. Unlike many other "sports," you don't have to subscribe to the traditional model of an athlete in order to have a shot at a career. With no random drug tests, no rules, and no training programs to adhere to, some people take it to the extreme, if you'll excuse the pun.**

When there's no coach telling you that you must turn up at 9am for practice, it's easy to allow yourself to sleep in after that wild party you went to last night. What are they going to do, fire you? Your boss was probably there and is no doubt doing the same thing you are right now: not getting out of bed.

So your day might get off to a slow start and you probably won't meet your buddies and teammates at the skate spot until about 2pm, after you've shaken off most of the hangover. Once you get there, because everyone is in the same hungover boat, you're not feeling any great pressure to do anything. However, if you've got an iota of self-determination, maybe you set yourself the challenge of filming a trick or shooting a photo, provided the spot offers an obstacle suited to your skills.

After a few hours, the session probably is in full swing—the homies are shredding, you got your trick after a bit of a battle, and the mood is high. This is when things will go one of two ways. The first is you take that positive energy and use it to carry on until you run out of steam, then get an early night so you can skate tomorrow. The second is you start the night early.

If you're a drinker, not much beats the good feeling of being at a secluded spot and sharing a few celebratory beers with your friend as the evening sets in. And if you're a hard drinker you might find that act of enjoying a beer begins to creep away from evening and further and further back toward the mid-afternoon, maybe even as far back as lunchtime.

When the sun is high in the sky and your head is thumping from last night's shots, you think it might just do to try the hair of the dog. You know, just to clear your head. However, if it gets to the point that you're drinking every night and this remedy becomes habit, you might want to consider taking some time out. Or seeking help. And if you start having your "lunch" at 9am, it's a must.

The trouble with all this boozing is that the lifestyle is glamorized a lot within skateboarding. There are role models left and right that seem to be high-functioning drinkers; guys who have no trouble downing beers at all hours of the day. These capable-looking few are the only alkies you will see footage from, making it look like all drunk skaters can pull shit out the bag while being shit-faced at the same time. All the useless drunks ain't out there getting tricks so you never notice them.

Drink is a problem for far more people than it isn't, something worth remembering when you're sitting there trying to remember a time when you went skateboarding when you weren't loaded. Maybe it's time for a little detox period, eh?

# THE MOSHER

**Heavy metal and the rock 'n' roll attitude has always had a close relationship with skateboarding. The don't-give-a-shit lifestyle of the Mosher works quite well with the way the average skater treats his body in pursuit of his art. That and the riffs are good.**

Often, the life of a skateboarder revolves around spending as little money as possible. Sleeping on couches, washing irregularly, traveling light, and partying all night—whether you like it or not—are prerequisites. And, to be honest, any metaller worth his or her salt should be doing the same. So it seems the two scenes are destined to intertwine. Sooner or later skaters and metallers will find themselves being put in the same bag by the Man and demonized as immature, anti-social menaces.

It's not too surprising then that there are more than a few metallers who skateboard. They can be identified easily by their varying degrees of devotion to rock—from the "I-own-one-Creedence-T-shirt" guys to the "never-out-of-black" long hairs that populate skateparks and murky street spots the world over. There is a distinction to make here and that is that to true Moshers skateboarding and heavy metal are on a level peg in terms of importance to their lives.

In addition to the fashions of rock, this proximity to the darker side of music often produces a strange and notable style of skateboarding. Big drop-ins seem to be the main area in which a Mosher professes. For him, the taller the drop he's attempting and the flatter the landing, the better—it means more impact to the knees. Grabs are always worth adding to a trick for good measure; nothing says Mosher like a good old stink-bug grab where none is truly needed.

Not all metallers are built for this kind of high-impact skateboarding though, and sometimes those ankle-length leather jackets make these drops near impossible. Even if the studded leather bracelets tell you he's about to get gnarly, don't be shocked if this guy instead starts doing weird flatground maneuvers that you've never seen.

The flatground Mosher's trick bag is mainly comprised of moves like boneless-one variants and stationary flip tricks. While not the most high-octane stunts, they are oddly impressive to watch, this is mostly down to the fact that these guys have no reference to learn from. They are probably having to make it all up as they go along because instead of religiously watching skate videos, they've been intently studying words to Pantera songs. This is what happens when kids are exposed only to the dork-around skating that people like Bam Margera do in mainstream programs like *Jackass*, not to the rich history that is offered in core skate movies.

The loner/warrior spirit that a lot of nerdy metallers display might make it difficult truly to get to know a Mosher, but they're always entertaining to watch as they try their gnarly or bizarre tricks.

# SKATE TRIPPERS

**Spend long enough in one place and you're going to get bored. Skateboarding is no different: if you frequent one spot long enough, it's only a matter of time before you're going to find yourself seeking out fresh terrain to try new tricks on.**

The ultimate high point in most any skateboarder's year is the skate trip. It could be something as simple as spending two days in a town an hour's drive away, or perhaps a massive spend of your whole year's earnings and a month off work going apeshit in Barcelona (yes, it's still that good over there).

Aside from the obvious benefits being abroad brings with it— the apparent allure of your accent to members of the opposite sex, the exotic food, and the better spots—the destination and format of a skate trip is kind of irrelevant, to be honest. The soppy, emotive posters in train stations and bus stops are right: it's the journey that's important, not the destination.

Unless you've got the cash to splurge on that flight abroad, your trip most probably will consist of a car full of you and your friends going as far as you can in the time you've got. Whatever your route, whatever the crew, and whatever the air-con situation, it's going to be hot and cramped in there. Space is at a premium and every available gap will be filled with shoes, boards, and sleeping bags. Calling "shotgun" is a skill worth learning.

If you don't secure the roomy seat up front, get one next to the window, otherwise you're not going to be able to evade the fetid stench of sweaty, farty air. In case you thought you were going to be able to dodge the stink by washing regularly (which will probably be impossible on your budget), there will be frequent stops at gas stations where everyone can top up the levels of rancid air with smelly junk food.

Although this situation is bad for you, your friend with the driving license is the worst off. As well as the stink of everyone's poor hygiene and diet, he's the one fronting all the cash on the gas and also the one who has to try and get you guys to pay him back. He'd be able to share the driving if anyone else had passed their test, but skateboarding and driving licenses don't really seem to go hand in hand.

Then there's the accommodation, which definitely won't be five-star luxury. At best you're going to be sleeping on the floor of friends' places or in cheap roadside motels. This all might not sound ideal, but the experience isn't about comfort and money. The whole point of this trip is skateboarding and you're going to enjoy yourself as long as you keep this thought at the forefront of your mind. If you can mange this, you'll forget all the horrible, smelly, terrible bits and remember the good times. Enjoy these, because soon you'll be back at work daydreaming about doing it all again.

# DIY Guy

So you've been skating this spot for years and suddenly you're getting kicked out daily by the cops, all because you're out having a good time on your board. What the hell's going on? It's not like you can go to the skatepark: it's crap, it's full of kids on scooters, they make you wear a helmet, and you can't even have a beer after the session is done. This isn't what you signed up for, something's got to be done. Time to take things into your own hands. Time for some DIY.

## Location

The first thing you're going to need is a place to build your spot. It's got to be the right place though. If you get it wrong, you're going to wind up getting arrested or, worse, losing it before you manage to finish it up!

Under bridges is always a popular choice for gnarly bowls and abandoned foundations tend to be popular with ledge skaters, but it's kind of up to you. I mean, that's why you're doing this, right? But if there's a water source nearby for mixing concrete and you can drive your car right up to it to drop off building materials, you're going to have way less of a hard time getting the spot going. It pays to think it through a little.

## Crew

Unless you're superman, you're going to need help to get this thing going. Lifting heavy bags all day on your own isn't fun, and, more's the point, this ain't going to be cheap! You're going to need people to cough up some cash for cement, for beers, and for charcoal. If they pay up, you guys can start making it quicker, drink while you work, and eat burned burgers after; plus they'll have earned the right to skate it.

Things might work even quicker if you can sweet talk a driver into dumping some of his leftover concrete from a job at your spot. If you try and find some cement that fell off the back of a truck, you'll save some cash. It might help if one or two of the guys you've recruited has worked with concrete before, once you've started mixing this stuff, there's no turning back.

## Naming

Every DIY spot needs a name, it's the rules. And naming that spot is the prerogative of the guys who make it. You might just consider using the suffix "side" on the place name, in honor of the Stonehenge of DIY parks: Burnside in Portland. If you're lucky, you might have a friend who's good at naming things, or there's something glaringly obvious and unique about the place that lends itself to a name. Just make it catchy if you want it to stick. There aren't really any rules here though, you're in charge, just make sure that if it's not clever that it's funny.

## Policing

So you and your bros have put time, money, and effort into this project and now you've reached the tricky situation of deciding who can and can't use it. One of the key elements of skateboarding is the appropriation of space, so it seems natural to most people that if it's there, then you can skate it. However, seeing as how long and hard you slaved over building this spot, you might find this idea doesn't sit well with you. DIY parks are notorious hovels of opinion and bitterness, so feel free to run with that.

The reality is that sometimes there's a troll under the bridge and that sometimes you might be better off paying a fare to the troll to appease him. What I'm saying is that you might want to think about asking random kids who turn up to donate a bag of cement, a few coins, or say half a case of ice-cold beer every now and again instead of throwing a half brick at them...

## Destruction

The unfortunate reality for a lot of DIY spots is that they have a limited lifespan. Most of them sit on the wrong side of legal, so that's kind of to be expected. Regardless of how redundant the space you've chosen is, someone—be it the city, the cops, or some asshole do-gooder—might just decide that your spot has to go. You're having too much fun, being too creative, and showing too much initiative to be allowed to continue. Go home and turn on your games console, like a good little drone. What are you going to do about it? Cry like a baby? Whaaa! This is what happens. Get used to it.

## Rebuilding

Provided you haven't just given up, become a gamer, or made your weary way back to the skatepark, helmet in hand, you might want to try and take what you've learned about your time spent at *insert-clever-play-on-words-here*-side and build on it (sorry). You're going to have to find yourself another spot and begin the whole process again, but the thing to remember is this time your spot will be built better, you'll be sneakier, and you'll be more passionate about it than ever. And think about all the good times there are to be had drinking beers, talking shit with your bros long into the night while you're waiting for that concrete to harden.

## Aftermath

Provided you've had a run of luck and your park's survived the local redevelopments, cops, and nosey neighbors, you're going to start thinking of this place as your home. You wake up and go there; you eat, drink, and skate there... You might as well be sleeping there. I mean, why exactly are you paying rent when you're never at your house? This is home now. Time to find a couch and a bed. Even better, make yourself one.

# COMPANY OWNER

**Ever wanted to make your own skateboards and set up your own company? Of course you have... You and all the other skaters on the planet. That's the problem, every Tom, Dick, and Harry who skates wants the same, so join the line.**

When setting up your own company, it used to be that you had to do it all yourself, and that ain't easy. Now things aren't quite so difficult—you can buy blank decks and even make a screen to print them in your own bedroom—but if you really want to make a go of it, you have to be prepared to work pretty hard. And be warned, even in this modern, Internet-fueled world margins are thin thanks to a recession that's left everyone broke as hell, so good luck with it. Still, some skaters with the necessary good ideas and drive to put in the long hours manage to make it work. But never mind the success stories, let's get to the problematic bits. It's what you want to hear, right?

One real problem is that some people seem to think it's okay to skate for a decade or two and then start up a company, stop skating, and get fat. Categorically the worst things you will hear in your life as a skateboarder—outside of the dull click of a ankle bone snapping inside your body, or the banshee screech of your wheels as a rogue stone abruptly stops your forward motion—has to be the phrase, "Hey, I used to skate..."

The culprit could be the cop who's trying to be cool about kicking you out of the spot, man, or it might be your friend's dad boring you with some tale from the late 70s. It could even be someone you just met who thinks you care about who they are or what they used to get up to in their spare time. I used to shit myself every day when I was in diapers, but this shared pastime doesn't mean we're friends or have anything in common, buddy!

But back to the point: the worst of the worst is when the idiot saying that dreaded line is the plump guy making all that fresh skate gear. His crime cannot be dismissed merely because he stuck around skateboarding for a few years before packing it in. If anything, that's far worse.

So, next time you meet a guy who works in the industry, check his waistband for gut overspill, check his shoes for holes, and when you shake their hand, be on the lookout for the lack of grip tape thumb. After all, it's your duty as a skateboarder to catch out quitters and expose them for what they are!

Respect those who live and breathe (and actually commit the act of) skateboarding despite having decided they'd like to make a living from it. Respect them as much as you despise the ones who gave it up. These dedicated few are the exalted ones. So make sure you support your local company owner.

# THE MILLIONAIRE

**This guy is a true product of the modern age of skateboarding. Ten years ago, the concept of someone wealthy enough to feature on a rich list being a skateboarder would have been laughable— they were thousandaires not millionaires. Now it seems they are ten a penny.**

If you've got talent enough to be able to make your millions by simply messing about on a wooden toy, you're either pretty lucky or you're really hard working and focused, or maybe both. However you got there, being super rich and being a skateboarder is a lifestyle most of us won't have the pleasure of experiencing unless our numbers happen to come up in the lottery, which makes these guys pretty hard to sympathize with. I mean, all you have to do is browse their social media for five minutes to discover they're living on a different planet. One where the new rims on a car or a shiny new gold medallion are deemed important enough to share with the world.

For anyone who's skated for longer than 15 years, the concept of being a super-rich skater died with the brash neon and board-sale percentage deals of the 80s. Even then the amounts earned were a world away from the riches amassed by this growing sub-sect of our beloved underground activity.

This modern-day capitalist creation has the likeness of a baseball, basketball, or hip hop star—a kid who rises from the gutter (for the most part) to a lifestyle so lavish even diamond-encrusted rappers consider it a little bit flashy. But these guys are young, so what the hell do they do with all that money? What would you do if you were 21 and earning more than both your parents combined? Unsurprisingly, it's not all philanthropy and charitable donations, it's a little more material than that.

The strange thing you do see these days is that the Millionaire's possessions are more and more likely to be locked up in non-depreciable investments like diamond earrings, trust funds, and dream houses.

The days when a skateboarder might squander his winnings on a beachfront rental he couldn't really afford, all-night parties with models, and a drug habit he couldn't handle are fairly well behind us. We are in an age of personality-sensitive million-dollar shoe deals, sports agents with bottom lines, personal physiotherapists, and a general focus on "career skateboarding." Where once you knew it was the kids making money and having fun with it (read: blowing stacks of cash on having a good time), there is a sense these days that someone is behind the scenes making life choices for the successful skaters, an advisor setting up their retirement plans, and making sure the money doesn't get wiped out doing dumb shit like turning up to demos in helicopters or emptying penthouse-suite mini bars with the homies. But you know what, skateboarding seems kind of weaker for all this PC stuff. I think I preferred it when people were blowing their cash— the stories were definitely better.

# SKATE WIDOW

**Skateboarding is still a pretty male dominated activity. I think only about five percent of those who practice the "sport" are girls. While this figure is changing for the better year on year, the sheer number of guys taking part means there are other-halves the world over being dragged by partners into the culture, whether they like it or not.**

To the young, the fact their female friend might be less interested in skateboarding than them doesn't always register. Like everything when you're a kid, it is certainly less of a concern. Ignorance is bliss. The fact they are a skater might have won them the girl's attention in the first place, so they bring her along in an effort to show off in front of her and her friends and to demonstrate to her what a cool thing it is that they do.

As time progresses, this poor girl will realize that for 90 percent of the time people spend skateboarding, they aren't making tricks, which is kind of boring to watch. This isn't helped by the fact there are no girls to talk to, the boyfriend is more interested in his board than you, and unless you skate, there's jack shit to do. You can

notice a girl has reached this state by the increased attention being paid to her cellphone, maybe a well-developed smoking habit, and possibly even wandering eyes. The main thing to take from this is that if, as a kid, you are relying on your talent to keep a girl interested in you, you will need to work a lot harder to hold onto her when you bring her to a spot that's rammed with more talented, older, bigger guys.

As you get older, you might realize that there are far more girls who aren't hanging around skateparks and skate spots than there are sat by the bowl or the four-set or stairs. Provided you're not a social outcast or creep, you might even find yourself dating one of them (lucky you!) but your troubles aren't over yet—it's just the beginning. This stranger to the skatepark might not get the fact you're used to spending all day hanging out with your friends. She might not appreciate that you're most likely not going to be back in time for dinner, that when you do show up, you'll be a sweaty mess, and you'll probably have at least a couple of friends in tow.

On the rare evenings when you aren't crashed on the couch talking in cryptic skate slang to your bros as she attempts to ignore the video you've put on, you might be out partying, and with any luck she'll want to come out and have a good time with her boyfriend. Eventually, though, she'll realize that attending the parties you go to means you'll probably be hanging out with more skateboarders, talking about skating, and leaving her out of the conversation. Unless you can see your way to paying her some attention, she might well consider looking somewhere else for her kicks. This is fair enough, you skate bore.

The life of a skate widow can be a frustrating one, so my advice would be to make sure you are capable of having a conversation with your girl about something else on occasion. Music, politics, movies, books... Anything but skateboarding.

# SPONSOR-ME KID

**Some people are just naturally good at skating and kids not blessed with the same gifts naturally look up to them, often purely because they're sponsored. The older you get, the less important getting a little free shit becomes, but to some kids, that's what they want in life more than anything.**

Ever since skateboarding was established, companies have sought out talented sportsmen to promote the activity. It's a model that all other sports share so it's not that surprising. Superstars endorsing your company make your product look better to fans of that superstar, meaning you sell more shit. Happy days.

In the era of short shorts, these skateboard superstars had to prove themselves and confirm they were worth the money by establishing and maintaining high contest placings. The model of obtaining a recognized ranking to secure endorsement remained fairly unchanged until the first major cultural shift affected the sponsorship game: the video. Once people realized that you didn't have to conform to the competition model in order for potential backers to take notice, things became infinitely more accessible, opening up the sponsorship game to any kid whose mom and pop had a handycam and a driveway to practice on.

As a skateboarder, the desire to get sponsored is a fairly unbalanced deal. You put in hours, sometimes days of effort to land that one life-changing, ankle-roll risking move on tape, then repeat the process long enough to gather together two minutes of footage. Next you put a soundtrack over the top and send it off to your favorite companies in the hope that someone sees it for long enough to take notice of your talent and likes you enough to want to give you a few planks of wood a year. The small returns on offer to the kid who is spotted don't seem to matter at all though, because it's a start. And if he is lucky enough to have only bagged that shop sponsor (offering 10 percent off shirts and one free board a year), the only way is up.

Eventually, the Sponsor-Me Kid is going to have his eyes set on getting free boards directly from a board company, which means he needs to prove himself even more. By now he will have realized his dad's camera footage isn't going to cut it and will have roped in a friend to film him going hard at all the local spots. Now he wears his shop sponsor with pride and makes trick gathering the entire focus of his skateboarding. Unfortunately, this can be a little boring to be around.

There is one major issue with all this effort: often a "career" in skateboarding is about skating well while appearing not to be trying very hard. Paradoxically, it can also be about looking like you're trying really hard not to fall off your board and getting away with it. Well, it's about looking good while you're trying hard, even though you are talented and it comes naturally. Oh yeah, it also involves not caring about all the sponsorship deals you've been offered and have accepted. Hard to figure out? Kind of. Not really though, just be yourself.

When you go skateboarding, if you care too much, people can tell. If you try too hard, people won't care. If you look like you're not trying hard enough, people won't care. If you're hanging on for dear life and making it look good people will care. It's kind of like a sixth sense, an unwritten rule, a thing you'll feel that cannot be taught. It's a failsafe to keep the sport looking good and stay legitimate.

So if you've got your sights set on being the best, you might want to consider focusing that desire inward, avoiding the trends and fashions, ignoring what other people think, and only skateboarding for yourself. Choose this way and things are probably far more likely to work out for you.

# THE LONE WOLF

Some people just aren't socially adept—they are reclusive and that's the way they like things to be. Their persona is internalized, they are probably used to getting mocked for being quiet, and they are also the ones who might snap if you push them too far.

For the most part, skateboarding is a social sport—chatting shit, learning tricks, teaching others, and sharing jokes are all a fairly fundamental part of most peoples' skateboard experience. But not all skaters are alike and to some it is a completely introverted and singular experience.

Rather than learn by example, to progress the Lone Wolf needs the focus you can only get from being alone. He practices his trickery like some sort of meditation, perfecting his moves on a farm in the middle of nowhere or on lonesome driveways the world over. Filling his journals with notes about foot placements and recording technical data, he keeps a reference of things like the perfect speed for the double flip and the importance of using specific muscle movements for certain tricks.

How did he get this way? Well, the Lone Wolf most likely grew up as an only child, one raised in relative isolation with a life that had plenty of room for practice. His knowledge of skateboard history is likely to be insanely impressive, and he's able to outshine yours. This is due to the attention paid to the videos he studied as a teenager, when he relentlessly analyzed skater's foot placements for each trick and tried to figure out how he, too, could replicate the move and maybe even improve it.

Without any skateparks or friends to hit the streets with, a Lone Wolf may well have developed into a Freestyler (see page 16). This kind of skateboarding doesn't require space or friends in order to work. This can be seen in modern day freestylers who neither move nor have friends. In fact, they might be the best example of a Lone Wolf.

However, there is a rare breed of isolationist that doesn't conform to this nerdy persona. You might find him roaming the back streets like some sort of feral beast. Unshaven and incapable of holding a conversation with anyone, this type of skateboarder prefers to be alone for very different reasons. The word we are looking for is intolerant. Intolerant of you, your opinions, what you stand for, and what you say and how you say it. You and everyone around you annoy this guy, he'd hate you if he could be bothered. The only pleasure he can find in his life is skateboarding, and in his opinion doing it with anyone other than himself just ruins it.

If you are of a delicate disposition, approach this one with caution, because he will speak his mind and he may well have a drink problem. Hell of a combo.

# THE WEEKENDER

**Part-timers are one of the most frowned upon of breeds in this pastime we call skateboarding. There is just no room for fair-weather skaters. A skateboard is for life, not just for Christmas.**

When it comes to the amount of time you spend on a skateboard, how much is enough? I mean, there are no rules, right? Wrong... I think. The question really should be how much is not enough?

The easiest way to find out if you're not as dedicated as you need to be is to ask yourself a few key questions to help figure it out. These simple self-checks, regularly employed, should ensure you keep yourself in the "lifer" category and continue to be a member of the great unscorned.

The first thing you need to ask yourself is, "What shoes do I have on?" If the answer is anything like brogues, Crocs, or flipflops, you are blowing it. Everyone knows skaters only wear skate shoes, and even then they will pontificate and argue about how much more legitimate the brand they've chosen is than the one their friend is wearing. Exceptions to this footwear rule are if you're at work and you are required to dress like a Norm, or if you're wearing flip flops to try and sort out that skateboard trench-foot stench you picked up after not cleaning you feet properly. Under no circumstance should you, or anyone for that matter, be wearing Crocs.

The second thing to ask yourself is, "What's the weather like out there?" If the answer is, "Looks nice, let's take a stroll in the park," you are blowing it. If the sun's shining you should be going skating. In fact, as long as it's not pouring rain or blowing a tornado out there, you should be riding your plank. Even if that is at the cost of losing your shitty-shoed job, girlfriend, or source of income. If you're thinking about going skating, then allow yourself to be convinced to do otherwise, you had better have an excellent excuse, like a funeral or a wedding to go to. Even then you have to be sure you can't fit in a few hours on the curb outside the church beforehand. Come on, seriously?

The final question that will confirm whether or not you are a Weekender is, "When was the last time I went skating?"or "Where's my board?" If you even have to ask yourself either of these questions, then you are not doing it often enough, period.

If you are picking and choosing when you go skateboarding, you'd better hope no one finds out what a pussy you're being, because friends will disown you and children will mock you. Basically, without regular skate sessions your life isn't worth living, so enjoy your time eating ice cream on the beach, playing Frisbee in the park, or hanging out with your girl and her best friends, because next time you go skating and you get a shinner, you're going to be crying like a baby, wishing you had continued to pummel your board into your lower leg so you were used to the pain like everyone else. Cry me a river.

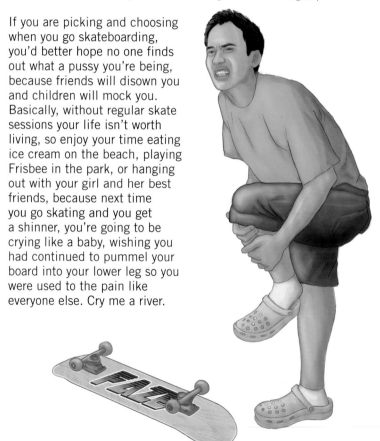

# TEAM EXTREME

**Indecision in the action sports world generally results in pain. Indecision about whether or not you've got the trick you're trying means a slam. Indecision about what device to choose to get your stoke on means alienation from every individual group and that can really, really hurt.**

The thing about skateboarding specifically is that it's the harshest of all the sports with regards to how it polices itself. For a "sport" without regulations, there are a surprising number of things that seem to look very, very similar to the things we know as rules. Not being one hundered percent committed to skateboarding, and only skateboarding, is one such heinous statute you may not think exists, but it does.

This rule is something that is hammered into a child's consciousness by the skate police from the moment said youngster turns up to the park/spot with more than one x-treme device. Skaters spend months of chipping away at a kid's lack of knowledge, continuously asking him, "What are you riding that thing for?" or bluntly sneering, "Get a board, man." They only engage the guy in conversation when he's riding his skateboard and pretend he doesn't exist when he stops to put on his blades.

The thing about a child who turns up to the park with the micro scooter, the blades, and the pennyboard is that by giving their kid such a degree of choice, his parents are only making it more difficult for him to improve his abilities and develop socially. An aspiring member of Team Extreme is never going to fit in with any crowd and never going to find any degree of solidarity unless he picks one discipline.

Instead, he will be a Jack of all trades and master of none, a half-ass, and no-one likes a half-ass.

It's a shame really because, as children, the innocence kids have, their willingness to try it all out for themselves, to find their own path, is most parents' dream. Allowing their child to have all the choice in the world is what all parents want, but the thing with moms and dads is that they are often oblivious to the problems other people have with their children. How could anyone harbor any ill will toward their little angel? Well, sorry to have to break it to you, but your kid annoys the hell out of me. Make him pick a version of extreme sports and stick with it. And that pick better be the skateboard or I know a few thousand people who will have an irrational dislike of your child. Forever.

# THE WANNABE GANGSTER

**Every local skate scene has at least one Wannabe Gangster. Dressed like an extra from BOYZ N THE HOOD and armed with a mean face and bad attitude, he thinks he's got something. What a dick.**

Skateboarding attracts all types of people from all kinds of backgrounds. That's part of the beauty of it, anyone can join in, no matter what color, class, or sexuality you are. But if you want to be respected by your peers and accepted into the fold, the one most important thing is that you are real. This is where the Wannabe Gangster fails to make the cut. The majority of skateboarders soon realize that you have to walk the walk as well as talk the talk. It's not about being the toughest or the best; it's about being yourself. This means Ecko jeans and fancy New Era hats are fine if that's what you're into, but if you are coming in hot, thinking you're the local skatepark's answer to Eminem, you might find you aren't going to make friends easily.

If someone thinks they're gangster, it means they're going to have attitude, which is a tool people outside of skating use when they feel threatened or offended. A Wannabe Gangster will usually be insulted by something insignificant or trite and their hair-trigger reaction is often a waste of energy that could be better used for skateboarding—if they ever actually did any.

Fashion is another waste of energy the WG could do without. Waking up in the morning means having to find the cap, doo-rag, and sneakers to match the basketball top. He then has to Instagram his joint and make sure he doesn't break a sweat on the way to the park. Dressing like an idiot can be hard work, but the real mission for any guy who thinks he's more G than he is will be keeping secret all the real-life shit he's concealing under the thugged-out lie. The 2.5-children family, the stable parents, the middle-class upbringing with plenty of love and attention, and the huge house in the fancy neighborhood could bring a faker's made-up world crashing down at any moment.

If the WG is really trying to pull the wool over everyone's eyes, he needs to be either selling weed or have a fledgling rap career. Or both. The drug-dealing smokescreen doesn't have to be a lucrative venture—mom and pop have got his back financially (although they do wish he'd grow up and get a job)—dime bags of shitty weed sold here and there for no profit will keep him looking legit on the streets. The rap career is an even easier tool to maintain the façade with, because it's merely more attitude and fakeness, both of which he's got in spades. Plus, who listens to rappers that are just starting out anyway?

There is the possibility this guy might one day clean up his act and get a real job when he realizes no-one believes or cares about who he's pretending to be.

Sadly, until then you're stuck with this fake-ass, clown-looking idiot who believes his own hype. God save you.

# THE CHAMELEON

**Skateboarders like to think they're the best. They sanctimoniously pride themselves on accepting people regardless of faith, color, and creed. They arrogantly believe they lead the trends when it comes to fashion and being "cool." The reality, for the most part, is they're all just a bunch of badly dressed social misfits with high opinions of themselves and jaded views, but hey...**

So you've started skating and even though everyone says, "Just be yourself," what they really mean is, "Whose gang are you going to join and where will you fit in?" Maybe you're one of the few people who have always known who you are and feel genuinely comfortable just being yourself, but my guess is you'll eventually cave in and try to fit in with a group. It's possible you could be the only straight-edge emo kid who rolls with the G'd-out weed heads, but unless you change up your style a little, my money's on you getting left out the crew.

How do you go about fitting in? One option is to adopt the chameleonic approach, a technique you could also call "testing the water." This process involves trying out a few different styles and groups of new friends to see what works best for you. Believe it or not, it can all be done on a budget. You could start with a cheap pair of baggy jeans, ones so big your ass hangs out. This should fit in with the Hip-Hop Guys, but you'll need to keep your shit pretty clean-and-fresh looking, so throw on some sports tops and whatever headgear is on trend. Gotta stay on the crest of the wave with these guys—it's all about the look.

If that seems like too much effort, just let it all go to pot and hang with the Dirty Grunger Kids. Now you can combine your new jeans with whatever crap you own, stop washing, and leave your hair to do whatever. Just be warned: whichever crew you choose, when you get older, you're probably going to be embarrassed about looking back at just how much boxer short was hanging out. Then again, humility isn't such a bad thing.

If you've grown tired of hiking up your baggy pants every two minutes, it might be time to tighten them up a little. Just be aware that if you tighten too far it could fire you right into another couple of elite groups, because super-tight pants mean one of two things: Rocker/Punker or Team Handsome. Opting for the latter gang is increasingly popular the world over, with kids rolling skin-tight jeans unnecessarily high above a simple pair of sneakers, presumably as a precaution for potential flash floods.

If you choose the handsome route, you'll need to take good care of your style, making sure you've got a few couture items in your quiver. Thankfully, the white v-neck T-shirt can be as dirty as you like, to show just how hard you skate and to remind people you don't really care what you look like, except you do.

The main downside to adopting this fashion is the pricey cigarette-and-take-out-coffee habit you'll need to maintain in order to appeal to all those model chicks who'll be hanging around you, trying not to eat lunch.

If this group seems a little uptight and impenetrable, you can always unfurl those turn-ups, splash out on a vintage leather jacket, and, hey presto, you're a Rocker! Remove the shirt; now you're a Punker— easy! There's a lot of middle ground here, so you can always tone it down a couple of notches. Plus you might get too old to want to be dressing up all the time; that shit can get to be tiring. Maybe you should just be yourself and focus on skating.

# THE MODEL

**In case you weren't paying attention, skateboarding is bigger than ever. This current popularity brings with it interest from other industries, like fashion, for instance. Companies that see fit to charge a small fortune for a T-shirt in their boutiques are now using skateboards to sell handbags and the like, which is unheard of in past skate history.**

If you're using skateboarding to sell fashion, why not use skateboarders as models, right? Now, just because some fashion designers have cottoned on to the fact "street style" sells doesn't necessarily mean they want you to show them how it's done. But if you've got a six pack, a strong jaw bone, and immaculate designer stubble, you might find yourself on course to a job getting paid simply for wearing clothes and hanging out with all those ridiculously skinny, good-looking girls.

So how do you get started as a model? To be honest, I don't know, but I'm willing to have a good crack at a guess. The first thing you're going to have to do is to get a haircut. I'm not talking any old trim at your local barber, you have to pay some real money for this—speculate to accumulate. Stylewise, think something foppish and on trend, at time of press the "slick back" is the cut of choice.

To match that perfect head of hair, you're going to need a good line of disaffected, nonplussed, middle-distance stares. Paying for a good black-and-white portfolio shoot should help here, and any fashion photographer worth his or her salt knows that look: moody, sultry, and not bothered.

Now you've got the face sorted and, provided you've accounted for the cigarette permanently being smoked, coffee permanently being clutched, and brandless-white-v-neck trifecta of cool, you're well on your way to becoming a model. But, as with all things, it's who you know not what you know, which means it's time you started meeting some other models. It looks like you're going to have to move to New York, LA, or London and get partying, because everybody knows the fashion industry loves that shit, right?

If you're one of the lucky few to get picked out of the crowd and make it to the glossy pages of a fashion magazine, you might find your skater friends take you less and less seriously. Unless, of course, you can still find the energy to get out of bed after that cocaine hangover and go and skate with some buddies.

With any luck, you're good enough at skateboarding that people don't even care you get paid to pout like an asshole and stand around trying to look cool. Soon you'll realize it's tough looking this good all the time... Maybe a facial and a spa break could help?

# THE TRAVELER

**If skateboarding fulfils only one of its many claims, it's the fact that it broadens the mind by offering new experiences and opens people's eyes to new places. Most skaters have found themselves in a city they previously never thought they'd visit and the reason is usually skateboarding.**

Some people take traveling to another level, trying to spend more time on the road than off it. But you're not likely to get further than the next town without a little bit of money, and unless you're lucky enough to have a sponsor that can pay to fly you to another country or buy you that cross-country train ticket, you're going to have to save.

Realistically, that probably means getting a job without many prospects, something that you can pick up and drop as you see fit. It also probably means crashing on a mate's couch or even moving back in with mom and dad—if you can handle that. And you're going to have to learn to be thrifty, because if you're working your ass off for half the year and saving money, you're definitely going to want to try and spend the rest of the year doing exciting things, not just sitting on your ass at home going mad.

The first thing to learn about how to travel cheaply is that you need to know someone who knows someone. With any luck, a connection with that once-removed friend is enough of a link to get you a few nights on his couch. If you're very lucky, he'll also know somebody somewhere else who might be able to help you out, and so on and so on. The interconnectivity of skateboarding helps everyone get by at one point or another.

With all this freeloading, one thing worth remembering if you're ever planning on being invited back or looking to get recommended onward is to be a good guest. It pays to buy the occasional bottle of wine or roll of toilet paper, to offer to cook a dinner, to do the dishes, and to clean up after yourself.

Getting a phone that can connect to the Internet is a real money saver, too, especially if you're planning on phoning home at all. Also, you're probably going to be traveling alone now and again, so stock up on some good music. Or better yet, read a book and swap it out with someone when you're done.

Once you're on the road, you will no doubt experience cultures that aren't what you're accustomed to. If you find yourself able to handle these situations, you might go in search of stranger and stranger lands with more and more bizarre goings on. You will definitely meet hundreds of skateboarders and, if you're good enough, perhaps get some photos and tricks in media outlets that exist outside your usual bubble.

Some people even manage to make an entire skate career out of traveling—permanently living out of a bag and always moving on to the next city and the next scene. It might be a little lonely at times— it's definitely hard going—but you'll meet more people than you ever thought possible and more faces than you can possibly remember. Whatever happens, you're going to have loads of stories to tell your grandkids, that's if you can ever hold down a relationship long enough to actually mate, what with all that traveling you're doing.

# THE CLOWN

**Skateboarding attracts all types of people, usually those looking for an activity they can do when they want, with whoever they want. Most commonly it's the misfits that stick around the scene, which means skating can be pretty weird sometimes.**

If you're trying to make it as a skater, you've got to have something special, something that sets you apart from the crowd. Maybe your body is not made to be grinding gnarly 10-stair handrails, or you're not drunk-and-grizzly enough to hop fences and slash grind those tight backyard pools? Perhaps you're just a pretty average skater? Even so, you still want to make it as a skateboarder, so how's that going to work? Well, believe it or not, you can actually carve out a career in skateboarding simply by being a bit of an oddball and having OK skills on a board, you just have to decide to become the Clown.

Don't be fooled into thinking you don't have to try if you choose this path, it's going to be hard work to make it, so get ready. One thing you will immediately notice about the Clown is that his hair may not be normal in either style or color. The hairdo is merely an additional item of fancy dress, a prop to customize and mold to match whatever else he's wearing. It might be bright blue in a mohawk one day or a powerful red skinhead the next. It's pretty much guaranteed that, whatever the 'do looks like, it'll match the color of the ramp he's just repainted or at the very least will be identical to the tone of his clothes.

Most of the successful clown acts going on in skateboarding have gotten there through persistence with the thematic style of skateboarding, a mind for thinking outside of the box, bolstered with a vision of how the end product will look. Where some people put in the hard work, learning the latest progressive moves, these guys are focusing on aspects that may make a photo unique or entertaining. They spend hours making everything just as they want it before carefully putting it into action. Weird. The Clowns are there to make you laugh at the absurdity of a situation and the in-jokes rife within skateboarding. Their job is to make you smirk in disbelief that they worked so hard at creating a situation that looks the way it does.

However, the main area where Clowns invest a major amount of time and money—and display true skill— is when it comes to the variety of boards they create for the shoots. If you are considering becoming one of these entertaining sorts, you're going to need a whole host of bizarre creations that you can use in place of the standard popsicle-shaped skate deck. It ain't going to be easy though—fish tanks, dart boards, Perspex, beds of nails, guitars, even human beings are ABD, so you'd better start thinking hard.

If all else fails, just get naked and skate, seems to make most everybody laugh.

# TERMINOLOGY

**To an outsider, the words and phrases used by skateboarders might make you question whether they're speaking a foreign language. Here's a handy guide Norms can use for translation purposes.**

## Equipment & Tricks

**Deck:** The wooden thing you'll be standing on. Um, sorry: the seven-ply, heat-treated-in-a-Chinese warehouse piece of hand-crafted, professional-quality, Canadian maple you'll be riding.

**Wheels:** The round bits that help you to move but can also stop instantaneously should you encounter a tiny stone.

**ABEC:** A rating completely unrelated to the performance (but increases the cost) of your bearings, which help your wheel spin round so that when they get all rusty, they make a real tasty noise. The best remedy for this is to leave your board in a puddle for a several hours before storing it in a shed for a year or two.

**Wax:** It's wax; the stuff candles are made of. The stuff you're convinced you need to smear over every ledge you come across when you're a kid, but seem to manage fine without once you get a bit of weight under your belt.

**Grip Tape:** That rough black tape on the top of your skateboard that ruins your shoes, jeans, and jackets. It can also be the cause of "grip-tape thumb" if grabbed while aerial maneuvers are being performed. It may double up as a nail file for emergency ghetto manicures.

**The Ollie:** Come on, where have you been for the last 40 years?

**The Kickflip:** What every kid wants you to show them as soon as they find out you can do one. What every kid wants to show you as soon as they learn it.

**Gay Twist:** Aerial maneuver involving a fakie 360, or Caballerial, whilst grabbing "mute" and not the act of adding lime to the neck of your Mexican beer or lemon zest and soda to your whisky.

**900:** Two and a half lateral rotations of you and your board. Who are you? Tony Hawk? Chill out dude, maybe get your ollie dialed first!

**Slam:** The act of falling over while trying to master the art of skateboarding.

**The Scorpion:** The advanced slam in which you slide face first on your front, with your arms by your side and your legs arched over so that your feet nearly touch your neck. Variants include unconsciousness and chin splitting.

**The Credit Card:** Skateboard deck: 60 notes. Brand new sneakers: 80 bucks. Trip to the hospital with your testicles in a bag after "sacking" that rail: priceless.

**The Corpse Toss:** The act of attempting a gnarly trick while knowing the slam potential outweighs the likelihood of riding away. Also known as a "sack of potatoes" due to the immediate halt of lateral- or forward-motion of the skateboarder.

## Etiquette & Technique
**Snaking:** The act of going before it's your turn. One of the main things you'll find kids doing, usually more through ignorance than as a "fuck you." To clarify: snaking is OK sometimes (like when it's your friend doing it), but not all the time (when you don't know/like the person doing it).

**Headphones:** Things that people put in their ears so they can act like ignorant assholes. Things that people take out of their ears to say "Eh?" every time you try and speak to them. Things that play your shit music to "amp you up." Take 'em out!

**Spitting:** The thing only total dickheads do on the floor at the spot/skatepark. The thing that ruins your day when you step in it.

**Dropping In:** The act of entering a ramp by hanging the board on the top edge of the obstacle and standing on the tail before leaning into the transition. Also, the thing people who don't skate and can't even push think looks easy enough to try. The thing that ultimately ruins said person's day.

**Session:** The act of skateboarding with your bros, dude.

**Lurking:** Hanging around and doing nothing. Variants include talking shit about skateboarding, making claims about skateboarding, smoking weed, talking about smoking weed, drinking beer, and deep speculation about things like chem trails, Monsanto, and lizards.

**Communication:** Acceptable ways of saying hello to people down the park/local spot include: the fist bump, the slap-pound, the high five, and the handshake. Variations may include: the slap, slap-pound, and the handshake-to-hug (aka bro-hug/hip-hop hug). Under no circumstances should a greeting involve a bro-lock thumb clasp thing. Get a diablo, bro.

**Focusing:** The purposeful, calculated snapping of a perfectly fine deck due to a build up of frustration. An act angry young men seem to love doing. An act that ruins a poor kid's day.

**Props:** Cheers of encouragement to fellow skateboarders when they are ripping hard. Popular variants include: "You got this," "Next go," and "Dude, you almost had that one."

**Claims:** When you verbalize your desire to perform a stunt. Variants include: "Couch Claims" (those made from the comfort of your couch whilst watching a skate video) and "Beer Claims" (those made after the session whilst under the influence).

**Shitfoot (aka Mongo):** Pushing with your front foot instead of back foot. OK in switch, serious faux pas when done in regular.

## Useful Terminology
**Sick!:** Exaltation in the positive.

**Regular/Goofy:** One way/the other way (respectively).

**Switch:** The art of skateboarding the wrong way around.

**Fakie:** The wrong way around but stood like you would be if you were going the right way around.

**Frontside:** Skate action (rotations, grinds, and slides) which occurs to the front of one's person.

**Backside:** That chubby bit separating your back and your legs.

**Grom:** Young skateboarder.

**Used to be [good/pro/sponsored/the best]:** Old-ass guy you don't care about.

**Fruitbooter:** A rollerblader.

**Line:** The successive completion of more than one trick in a row. I know. Wow.

**Hammer:** A trick so good that people ignore the fact that you didn't do more than one trick in a row.

**ABD [Already Been Done]:** So don't bother trying it. Loser.

**NBD [Never Been Done]:** Not by these legs, at any rate.

**Buttery/Butters:** Description for the smooth, fluid, successful performance of a skateboard trick. i.e. "That shit was buttery."

**Stinking:** Description of a raggedy, sketchily performed trick. Often accompanied with a wafting motion or pinching of one's nose, i.e. "That shit was stinking."

# Index